Dandelion Rea

Reading and Spelling Activities
The Extended Code
Level 4

Phonic Books Ltd
www.phonicbooks.co.uk

Contents

Introduction — page 1

Dandelion Readers – Extended Code Series — page 2

This folder belongs to — page 3

Activities for Book 1, 'Toad and Newt' – spellings for 'ue' — page 4

Activities for Book 2, 'Fred Gets in Trouble' – spellings for 'u' — page 18

Activities for Book 3, 'Australia' – spellings for 'o' — page 32

Activities for Book 4, 'Five Excited Mice' – spellings for 's' — page 46

Activities for Book 5, 'Carrots and Celery' – spelling <c> — page 60

Activities for Book 6, 'The Camel' – spellings for 'l' — page 74

Activities for Book 7, 'The Ginger Cat' – spellings for 'j' — page 88

Activities for Book 8, 'George' – spelling <g> — page 102

Activities for Book 9, 'Steph, the Elephant' – spellings for 'f' — page 116

Activities for Book 10, 'A Grand Adventure' – suffix <-ture> — page 130

Activities for Book 11, 'The Inspection' – suffix <-tion> — page 144

Activities for Book 12, 'Viv's Profession' – suffixes <-ssion> <-cian> — page 158

Activities for Book 13, 'The Treasure Hunt' – suffix <-sure> — page 172

Activities for Book 14, 'Alien Invasion' — page 186

Blank reading game sheet — page 199

Introduction

Children learning to read with Synthetic Phonics learn to identify the letters (or groups of letters) in the English Phonic Code and the sounds they represent. They learn to blend the sounds together into words. This is called 'decoding'. They learn to spell by segmenting a word into its phonemes and using the correct spelling for these phonemes. This is called 'encoding'.

The English Phonic Code is a complex code and learning to decode and encode takes a great deal of practice. The worksheets in this pack offer a number of activities and games to develop decoding (reading) and encoding (spelling) skills. One of the difficult aspects of the English Phonic Code is that phonemes can be spelled in different ways. The Extended Code books in Levels 1, 2 and 3 teach this in a step-by-step progression. To see the structure of the three levels of books, see the table opposite.

The fourteen chapters in this workbook correspond to the fourteen books in the Level 4 series offering phonic work within the context of the stories.

Level 1 books introduce one spelling for each vowel sound e.g. the spelling <ai> for the sound 'ae'. These books complement any programme that teaches one spelling at a time e.g. 'Letters and Sounds'.

Level 2 books introduce two or three spellings for each vowel sound e.g. Book 1, 'Viv Wails' introduces the spellings <ai>, <ay> and <a> for the phoneme 'ae'. Level 2 complements any phonic programme that is teaching alternative spellings for a sound.

Level 3 books introduce four or five spellings for each vowel sound e.g. Book 1, 'Jake, the Snake' introduces <ai>, <ay>, <a>, <a-e> and <ea> for the phoneme 'ae'. These books complement any phonic programme that is teaching a number of alternative spellings. It is particularly suitable for catch-up pupils who need to learn at an accelerated pace. Some teachers may wish to work through the levels vertically, teaching one, three and five spellings within each phoneme, e.g. using Book 1 from Level 1, Book 1 from Level 2 and Book 1 from Level 3 before moving on to Book 2. The clear structure of the series allows for this.

Level 4 books introduce more complex spellings for vowels, consonants and suffixes. At this stage, the reader can be taught a number of suffixes (e.g. <-tion>) which come at the end of many words in English. These are taught as syllables which enable the pupil to read and spell many multisyllabic words with these endings.

The books and the activities can be used in any order. The teacher can use them while following the structure of any phonic programme being taught. The following reading and spelling activities include blending, segmenting and comprehension. Children learn best when they enjoy themselves. Two games have been included in each chapter for practice and consolidation at each stage. A spelling assessment concludes each chapter. The teacher can use this as an assessment tool. This list includes useful high-frequency words which are spelled with the target grapheme.

Dandelion Readers
Extended Phonic Code Series

Level 1

	Phoneme	Grapheme	Book
Book 1	ae	ai	The Mail
Book 2	ee	ee	The Tree
Book 3	oe	oa	Raj Gets a Soak
Book 4	er	ur	My Turn
Book 5	e	ea	Bread and Jam
Book 6	ow	ow	Mr Brown
Book 7	b'oo't	oo	Zoom!
Book 8	ie	igh	The Night Flight
Book 9	l'oo'k	oo	In the Wood
Book 10	or	or	The Fort
Book 11	oi	oi	Oil
Book 12	ar	ar	Too Far
Book 13	air	air	Fairy Wings
Book 14	ear	ear	Dear Old Friends

Level 2

	Phoneme	Grapheme	Book
Book 1	ae	ai, ay, a	Viv Wails
Book 2	ee	ee, e, ea	Sweet Dream
Book 3	oe	oa, o, ow	Toad Moans and Groans
Book 4	er	ur, er, ir	Meg Gets Dirty
Book 5	e	ea, e, ai	Raj Bumps his Head
Book 6	ow	ow, ou	The Tree House
Book 7	b'oo't	oo, ew, ue	The Blue Scooter
Book 8	ie	igh, i, y	I Spy
Book 9	l'oo'k	oo, oul, u	The Bush
Book 10	or	or, a, aw	Dan Draws a Monster
Book 11	oi	oi, oy	Roy, the Cowboy
Book 12	ar	ar, a, al	Trip to the Farm
Book 13	air	air, are, ere	Careless Fairy
Book 14	ear	ear, eer, ere	Max, the Meerkat

Level 3

	Phoneme	Grapheme	Book
Book 1	ae	ai, ay, a, a-e, ea	Jake, the Snake
Book 2	ee	ee, e, ea, y	A Heap of Sand
Book 3	oe	oa, o, ow, oe, o-e	Toad in a Hole
Book 4	er	ur, er, ir, or, ear	Pasta with Butter
Book 5	e, ae, ee	ea	The Mean Robot
Book 6	oe, ow	ow	Miss Flower's Project
Book 7	b'oo't	oo, ew, ue, u-e	School Rules
Book 8	ie	igh, i, y, ie, i-e	The Kite
Book 9	b'oo't, l'oo'k	oo	The Tooth
Book 10	or	or, a, aw, au, al	The Tent on the Lawn
Book 11	oi	oi, oy, uoy	The Royal Chest of Coins
Book 12	ar	ar, a, al, au, ear	Aunt March
Book 13	air	air, are, ere, ear, eir	Not Fair!
Book 14	air, ar, er, ear	ear	Bear's Fears

Level 4

	Phoneme	Grapheme	Book
Book 1	ue	ue, ew, u, u-e	Toad and Newt
Book 2	u	u, ou, o	Fred Gets in Trouble
Book 3	o	o, a, ou, au	Australia
Book 4	s	s, ss, se, c, ce, st, sc	Five Excited Mice
Book 5	s and k	c	Carrots and Celery
Book 6	l	l, ll, il, al, e, le, ol	The Camel
Book 7	j	j, g, ge, dge	The Ginger Cat
Book 8	j and g	g	George
Book 9	f	f, ff, gh, ph	Steph, the Elephant
Book 10	cher	-ture	A Grand Adventure
Book 11	shun	-tion	The Inspection
Book 12	shun	-ssion, -cian	Viv's Profession
Book 13	zher	-sure	The Treasure Hunt
Book 14	zhun	-sion	Alien Invasion

Dandelion Readers

This folder belongs
to

_____

www.phonicbooks.co.uk enquiries@phonicbooks.co.uk tel: 01666 822543 mob: 07711 963355

The Extended Phonic Code
Level 4 Book 1

'Toad and Newt' – ‹ue› ‹u-e› ‹ew› ‹u›

Blending with 'ue' spellings   page 5

Reading practice   page 6

Reading and spelling   page 7

Chunking two-syllable words with 'ue' spellings   page 8

Reading comprehension – find the untruths *   page 9

Punctuation exercise – capital letters and full stops   page 10

Non-fiction reading comprehension: Newts – true or false?   page 11

Write the story in your own words   page 12

Timed reading exercise   page 13

Dictation   page 14

Phonic patterns   page 15

Reading game   page 16

Spelling assessment 'ue' spellings   page 17

*4 untruths: They did not swim in the sea; Toad did not lose a leg; Toad was not in the shed; Newt did not fetch a rubber plug.

Blending with 'ue' spellings

ar	g	ue

s	t	ew

p	u	p	il

c	u	t	e

Blend the sounds into words. Draw a picture in the box to match each word.
<u-e> is presented on half squares as it is a split vowel digraph. © Phonic Books Ltd 2014

Reading practice

music	cue	news
argue	few	rescue
cube	tunic	pupil
student	stew	refuse
fumes	useful	Tuesday
confuse	unicorn	'ue' spellings <ue> <u-e> <ew> <u>

Reading and spelling

List the words according to the 'ue' spellings

ue	**ew**
_____	_____
_____	_____
_____	_____
_____	_____
_____	_____

u	**u-e**
_____	_____
_____	_____
_____	_____
_____	_____

cute   dew   pupil   pew   cube   due   mute   stew

use   knew   mutant   cue   cucumber   news   rescue

nephew   excuse   refuse   music   funeral

Chunking two-syllable words with 'ue' spellings

useful	use	ful	useful
newsroom			
pupil			
rescue			
amuse			
fewer			
Tuesday			
venue			
excuse			
nephew			
argue			
music			
refuse			
statue			

Split the word into two syllables. Write each syllable in a box. Write the whole word while saying the syllables. This sheet may be photocopied by the purchaser. © Phonic Books Ltd 2014

Reading comprehension - find the untruths

When Toad and Newt were little, they used to swim together in the sea. They both had tails, back then. Then they grew up and Toad lost a leg. One Tuesday in spring, he didn't want to go swimming with Newt anymore. Newt tried to get Toad out of his shed. It was no use! In the end, Newt ran home to fetch a rubber plug. Toad happily agreed to swim with the rubber tube.

There are **4** untruths in the story above. Can you spot them?

Punctuation exercise

Capital letters and full stops

toad and newt used to go swimming in the big pond then toad refused to go swimming with newt newt was sad and confused he tried to play him some music but it was no use

There are **7** capital letters and **4** full stops missing.
Did you spot them all?

Ask the pupil to read through the text and add in capital letters and full stops where necessary.
Encourage the pupil to read the text aloud as this will help him/her identify where the sentences stop.
This sheet may be photocopied by the purchaser. © Phonic Books Ltd 2014

Non-fiction reading comprehension

Newts - true or false?

The word **'predators'** means animals that kill other animals for food.

Newts are amphibians (am-phi-bi-ans). That means that they live in water and on land. They can breathe air and they can breathe underwater. The females are larger than the males. The females lay 400 eggs in the spring. Newts have poison in their skin to scare away predators. Did you know that, if a newt loses its tail, part of its spinal cord or an eye, it can grow back again?

	👍	👎
Newts live in water only.		
Newts can breathe underwater.		
The males are bigger than the females.		
Newts have poison on their skin.		
If a newt loses its leg, it will grow back.		

Ring the 'thumbs up' if the statement is true and the 'thumbs down' if it is not.

Write the story in your own words

In the beginning,

_____

_____

_____

_____

Then,

_____

_____

_____

_____

In the end,

_____

_____

_____

_____

Ask the pupil to retell the story orally before writing it.

Timed reading exercise

cute dew pupil few cube due mute stew use

knew mutant cue cucumber news rescue nephew excuse

refuse music funeral usual pew argue tunic confuse

accuse newspaper student statue tutor

| | 1st try |
| Time: | |

cute dew pupil few cube due mute stew use

knew mutant cue cucumber news rescue nephew excuse

refuse music funeral usual pew argue tunic confuse

accuse newspaper student statue tutor

| | 2nd try |
| Time: | |

cute dew pupil few cube due mute stew use

knew mutant cue cucumber news rescue nephew excuse

refuse music funeral usual pew argue tunic confuse

accuse newspaper student statue tutor

| | 3rd try |
| Time: | |

Dictation

Toad and __ ____ __   ____ __ ____ to swim in

the big __ __ __ __ when they were little.

One __ ____ __ __ ____ in spring, Toad

____ __ __ __ __ ____ to come out to play with

__ ____ __.

Newt did not want to ____ __ ____. He

__ __ ____ ____ Toad some __ __ __ __ __

to cheer him up.

In the end, __ ____ __ ran to fetch two

__ ____ rubber __ __ ____ __. Toad agreed

to float in the __ __ ____ pond.

Toad and N ew t u s ed to swim in the big p o n d when they were little.
One T ue s d ay in spring, Toad r e f u s ed to come out to play with
N ew t. Newt did not want to ar g ue. He p l ay ed Toad some m u s i c
to cheer him up. In the end, N ew t ran to fetch two n ew rubber
t u be s. Toad agreed to float in the h u ge pond.

Use the text at the bottom of the page for dictation. Fold the page on the dotted line. Dictate the
passage to the pupil. Ask her/him to spell the missing words, writing a sound on each line. Explain
that a longer line indicates a spelling with more than one letter e.g. n igh t. Ask the pupil to unfold the
sheet and check his/her spellings. This sheet may be photocopied by the purchaser.
© Phonic Books Ltd 2014

Level 4 Book 1: 'Toad and Newt' <ue> <u-e> <ew> <u>

Phonic patterns

Colour in the words with 'ue' spellings

understand	music	refuse	statue
argue	rubber	flute	blue
amusement	ruby	rescue	pupil
glue	useful	uniform	gutter
news	Tuesday	few	tune

Fold this sheet on the dotted line. Read the words in the column on the left. Listen to the sounds in the words. Colour in the lozenges with words that have 'ue' spellings. Repeat this in the other columns. Unfold the sheet and check the correct words have been coloured in.

This sheet may be photocopied by the purchaser. © Phonic Books Ltd 2014

Level 4 Book 1: 'Toad and Newt'

Reading game

\<ue\> \<u-e\> \<ew\> \<u\>

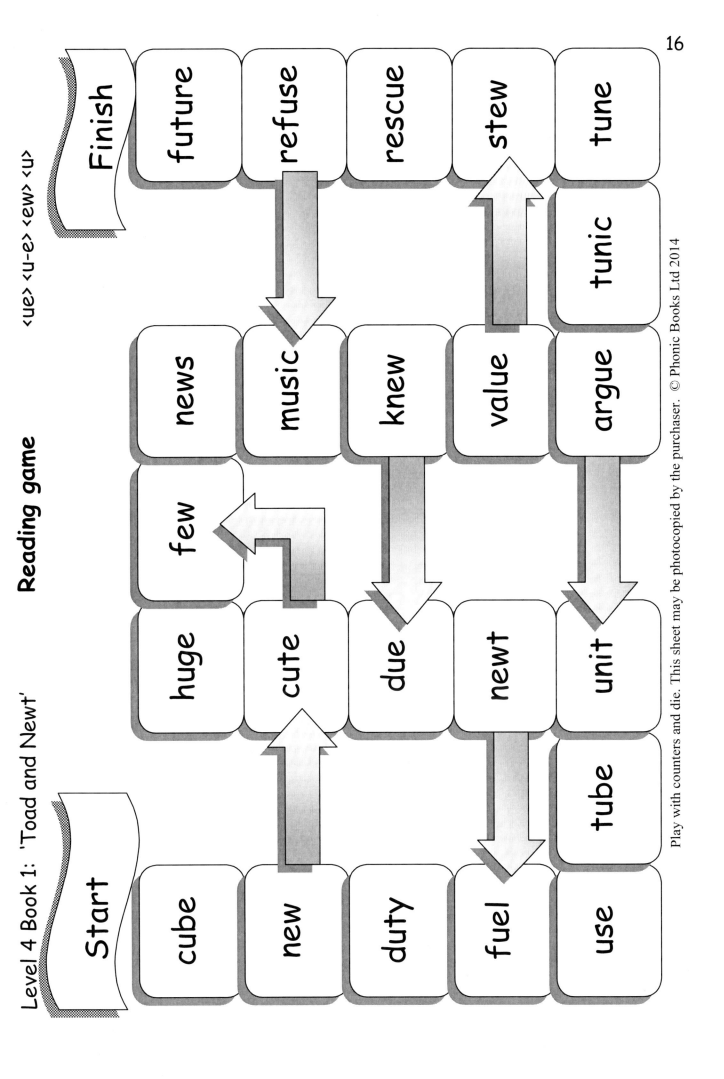

Start

cube new duty fuel use tube

huge cute due newt unit

few news music knew value argue tunic

future refuse rescue stew tune

Finish

Play with counters and die. This sheet may be photocopied by the purchaser. © Phonic Books Ltd 2014

Spelling assessment

1.

ue	ew	u	u-e
due	new	music	use
Tuesday	few	pupil	cube
rescue	stew	tutor	tube
statue	knew	unit	huge

- -

2.

ue	ew	u	u-e
venue	dew	tunic	refuse
avenue	nephew	cucumber	excuse
argue	curfew	funeral	accuse
		document	attitude
		unicorn	ridicule

This list can be used as a spelling assessment at the end of each unit of work.
The teacher can add words from list 2 for able pupils. When dictating a word, say the word.
Then say a sentence with the word in it (to put the word in the context of a sentence) and then repeat
the word. E.g. "Tuesday. On Tuesday, we went on a school trip. Tuesday". This ensures that the
pupil has heard the word correctly. The teacher can include homophones, e.g. 'new/knew' but will
need to explain them to the pupil.   This sheet may be photocopied by the purchaser.
© Phonic Books Ltd 2014

The Extended Phonic Code
Level 4 Book 2

'Fred Gets in Trouble' – <u> <ou> <o>

Blending with 'u' spellings   page 19

Reading practice   page 20

Reading and spelling   page 21

Chunking two-syllable words with 'u' spellings   page 22

Reading comprehension – find the untruths*   page 23

Punctuation exercise – capital letters and full stops   page 24

Non-fiction reading and comprehension : Recipe for chocolate
cornflake cakes - true or false?   page 25

Write the story in your own words   page 26

Timed reading exercise   page 27

Dictation   page 28

Phonic patterns   page 29

Reading game   page 30

Spelling assessment 'u' spellings   page 31

*The untruths: Mum and Fred did not bake the cake for Dad; Fred did not lick the cake; there were no buttons left on the cake; Mum did not put candles on the cake.

Blending with 'u' spellings

s	u	n	

d	o	ve	

y	ou	ng	

m	o	n	ey	

Blend the sounds into words. Draw a picture in the box to match each word.

Reading practice

ugly	cover	young
rough	nothing	among
until	country	courage
oven	worry	couple
touch	Monday	month
enough	none	'u' spellings <u> <ou> <o>

Reading and spelling

List the words according to the 'u' spellings

u
_____
_____
_____
_____
_____

ou
_____
_____
_____
_____
_____

o
_____
_____
_____
_____
_____

some   uncle   hunger   southern   worry   nothing

young   come   gutter   brother   month   sunk

trouble   touch   blunt   flourish   plump   country

Chunking two-syllable words with 'u' spellings

hundred	hun	dred	hundred
younger			
mother			
couple			
wonder			
sulking			
country			
nothing			
nourish			
Monday			
trouble			
custard			
honey			
southern			

Split the word into two syllables. Write each syllable in a box. Write the whole word while saying the syllables. This sheet may be photocopied by the purchaser. © Phonic Books Ltd 2014

Reading comprehension - find the untruths

Mum and Fred baked a cake for Dad's birthday. Mum put the cake in the oven. When it was ready, Fred went to check it and he touched it. Then he licked it with his tongue. He gobbled up one chocolate button, then another and another. There was one button left on the cake. Mum was cross and put candles on the cake instead.

There are **4** untruths in the story above. Can you spot them?

Punctuation exercise

Capital letters and full stops

fred helped his mum bake a cake for his brother mum put the cake in the oven fred went to check it he touched it and then ate one chocolate button after another what had he done?

There are **5** capital letters and **4** full stops missing.

Did you spot them all?

Non-fiction reading and comprehension
Recipe for chocolate cornflake cakes
True or false?

Ingredients
- 50g butter
- 100g milk chocolate broken into chunks
- 3 tablespoons of golden syrup
- 100g cornflakes

Method
1. Put butter, chocolate and golden syrup in a saucepan and melt on a low heat.
2. Put cornflakes in a big bowl.
3. Pour melted chocolate, butter and syrup over the cornflakes.
4. Stir the mixture gently with wooden spoon.
5. Divide mixture into 12 cupcake cases.
6. Put in fridge to set.

First, melt the cornflakes in a pot.	👍	👎
First, melt the butter, chocolate and syrup.	👍	👎
Next, put the cornflakes in the oven.	👍	👎
Next, pour the mixture over the cornflakes	👍	👎
Finally, leave in fridge to set.	👍	👎

Write the story in your own words

In the beginning,

_____

_____

_____

_____

Then,

_____

_____

_____

_____

In the end,

_____

_____

_____

_____

Ask the pupil to retell the story orally before writing it.

Timed reading exercise

some uncle hunger southern worry nothing couple tough

other young come gutter brother month sunk trouble

touch blunt flourish plump country mother rough son

another until double munch wonder younger dove

	1st try
Time:	

some uncle hunger southern worry nothing couple tough

other young come gutter brother month sunk trouble

touch blunt flourish plump country mother rough son

another until double munch wonder younger dove

	2nd try
Time:	

some uncle hunger southern worry nothing couple tough

other young come gutter brother month sunk trouble

touch blunt flourish plump country mother rough son

another until double munch wonder younger dove

	3rd try
Time:	

This timed reading exercise is for the pupil to improve his/her reading speed and fluency. Fold the page on the dotted lines. Ask the pupil to read the words as fast as they can. Record the time in the box. Repeat the exercise. This sheet may be photocopied by the purchaser.

Dictation

Fred helped his __ __ ____ ____ bake a cake for his

__ __ __ ____ ____, __ ____ __. Mum put the cake

in the __ __ __ __. When it was ready, Fred

__ __ __ ____ ____ the cake with chocolate

__ __ ____ __ __ __. Later, Fred went to

____ __ ____ the cake and ate one button after

__ __ __ ____ ____.

He was in big __ __ ____ __ ____!

Mum was __ __ __ ____. She quickly

__ __ __ ____ ____ ____ the cake with chocolate

__ __ __ ____ __. __ ____ __ __ __ __ ____ his

chocolate cake and so did his __ __ __ ____ ____!

Fred helped his m o th er bake a cake for his b r o th er, D ou g. Mum
put the cake in the o v e n. When it was ready, Fred c o v er ed the
cake with chocolate b u tt o n s. Later, Fred went to check the cake
and ate one button after a n o th er. He was in big t r ou b le! Mum was
c r o ss. She quickly s m o th er ed the cake with chocolate s p r ea d.
D ou g l o v ed his chocolate cake and so did his b r o th er!

Use the text at the bottom of the page for dictation. Fold the page on the dotted line. Dictate the
passage to the pupil. Ask her/him to spell the missing words, writing a sound on each line. Explain
that a longer line indicates a spelling with more than one letter e.g. n igh t. Ask the pupil to unfold the
sheet and check his/her spellings. This sheet may be photocopied by the purchaser.

Level 4 Book 2: 'Fred Gets in Trouble' <u> <ou> <o>

Phonic patterns

Colour in the words with 'u' spellings

rough	southern	route	hound
loud	around	sound	trouble
butter	bone	love	enough
gone	son	nothing	mother
worry	trust	touch	group

Fold this sheet on the dotted line. Read the words in the column on the left. Listen to the sounds in the words. Colour in the lozenges with words that have 'u' spellings. Repeat this in the other columns. Unfold the sheet and check the correct words have been coloured in.

This sheet may be photocopied by the purchaser. © Phonic Books Ltd 2014

Level 4 Book 2: 'Fred Gets in Trouble'   **Reading game**   <u> <ou> <o>

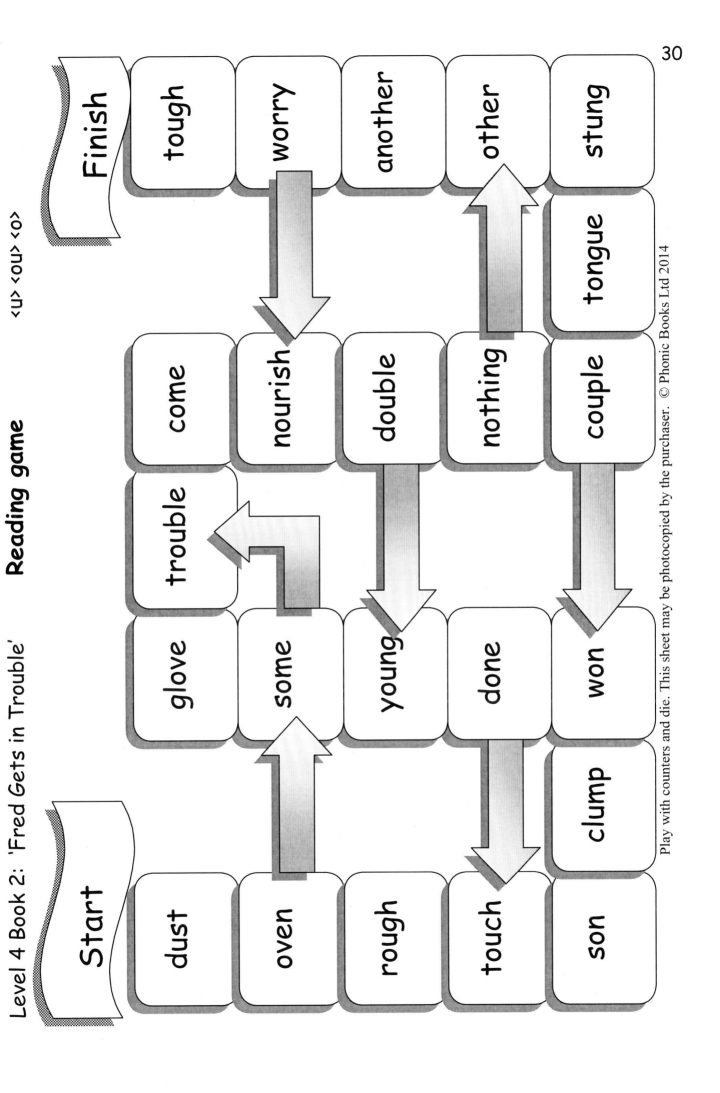

Spelling assessment

1.

u	**ou**	**o**
under	young	come
until	touch	some
ugly	cousin	love
sum	country	Monday

- -

2.

u	**ou**	**o**
hunger	couple	month
plump	courage	nothing
thumb	tough	other
		mother
		brother

This list can be used as a spelling assessment at the end of each unit of work.
The teacher can add words from list 2 for able pupils. When dictating a word, say the word.
Then say a sentence with the word in it (to put the word in the context of a sentence) and then repeat the word. E.g. "Tuesday. On Tuesday, we went on a school trip. Tuesday". This ensures that the pupil has heard the word correctly. The teacher can include homophones, e.g. 'sum/some' but will need to explain them to the pupil. This sheet may be photocopied by the purchaser.

The Extended Phonic Code
Level 4 Book 3

'Australia' – <o> <a> <ou> <au>

Blending with 'o' spellings   page 33

Reading practice   page 34

Reading and spelling   page 35

Chunking multisyllable words with 'o' spellings   page 36

Reading comprehension – find the untruths*   page 37

Punctuation exercise – capital letters and full stops   page 38

Non-fiction reading and comprehension:
Wallabies - true or false?   page 39

Write the story in your own words   page 40

Timed reading exercise   page 41

Dictation   page 42

Phonic patterns   page 43

Reading game   page 44

Spelling assessment 'o' spellings   page 45

*The untruths: Nan did not take Grandpa to the zoo; it was not cold in Australia;
Nan did not leave Grandpa behind.

Blending with 'o' spellings

w	a	sh	

d	o	t	

c	ou	gh	

s	au	s	a	ge	

Blend the sounds into words. Draw a picture in the box to match each word.
© Phonic Books Ltd 2014

Reading practice

want	squash	Austria
cough	because	wallet
trough	wander	washing
watch	wasn't	swallow
Australia	swan	wanted
sausage	wattle	'o' spellings <a> <o> <ou> <au>

Reading and spelling

List the words according to the 'o' spellings

a	o
_____	_____
_____	_____
_____	_____
_____	_____
_____	_____

ou	au
_____	_____
_____	_____
_____	_____
_____	_____

because   wallet   cough   trough   squash   wasp

Australia   plot   blogging   Austria   swallow   swap

sausage   trodden   squatted   wanted   was   drop

Chunking multisyllabic words with 'o' spellings

trotted	trott	ed	trotted
wanted			
squatted			
coughing			
because			
wander			
sausage			
wallet			
washing			
Austria			
swallow			
swapping			
watching			
squashing			

Split the word into syllables. Write each syllable in a box. Write the whole word while saying the syllables. This sheet may be photocopied by the purchaser. © Phonic Books Ltd 2014

Reading comprehension - find the untruths

Grandpa wanted to see wallabies in Australia. Nan looked at her watch and took him to the zoo instead. When they landed, they swapped their hats because it was cold. They had a picnic with sausages and salad. Then Grandpa fed the wallabies bits of salad. When the wallabies surrounded them, Nan got a bit nervous and coughed. She sped off in the Fab Cab and left Grandpa behind.

There are **3** untruths in the story above. Can you spot them?

Punctuation exercise

Capital letters and full stops

grandpa wanted to see wallabies in the wild he set off with nan to australia to see wallabies they landed and had a picnic grandpa fed the wallabies the wallabies got closer and closer

There are **7** capital letters and **5** full stops missing.
Did you spot them all?

Ask the pupil to read through the text and add in capital letters and full stops where necessary.
Encourage the pupil to read the text aloud as this will help him/her identify where the sentences stop.
This sheet may be photocopied by the purchaser. © Phonic Books Ltd 2014

Non-fiction reading and comprehension
Wallabies - true or false?

Wallabies belong to a family of mammals with pouches, called marsupials (mar-su-pi-als). They are born very tiny and they climb into their mother's pouch and find a teat in the pouch. They suck milk from their mother and live in the pouch for about one year. They are born blind and furless and are as big as a bean. As they grow, they begin to spend more time outside the pouch and they start to eat grasses and plants. The babies are called 'joeys'. Wallabies have very powerful back legs and tails. They use them to fight predators or each other.

Did you know a group of wallabies is called a 'mob'?

Marsupials are animals that have pouches.	👍	👎
Wallabies are born in their mother's pouch.	👍	👎
They are born with fur.	👍	👎
When they are born, they can see.	👍	👎
They live in the pouch for five years.	👍	👎
Wallabies use their legs and tails to fight.	👍	👎

Ring the 'thumbs up' if the statement is true and the 'thumbs down' if it is not.

Write the story in your own words

In the beginning,

_____

_____

_____

_____

Then,

_____

_____

_____

_____

In the end,

_____

_____

_____

_____

Ask the pupil to retell the story orally before writing it.

Timed reading exercise

was   because   want   swat   honk   wash   cough   sausage   wander

wallet   swap   golf   swan   trough   wasp   wand   wallow   Australia

squad   watch   what   swallow   Austria   squash   toddler

1st try
Time:

was   because   want   swat   honk   wash   cough   sausage   wander

wallet   swap   golf   swan   trough   wasp   wand   wallow   Australia

squad   watch   what   swallow   Austria   squash   toddler

2nd try
Time:

was   because   want   swat   honk   wash   cough   sausage   wander

wallet   swap   golf   swan   trough   wasp   wand   wallow   Australia

squad   watch   what   swallow   Austria   squash   toddler

3rd try
Time:

This timed reading exercise is for the pupil to improve his/her reading speed and fluency. Ask the pupil to read the words as fast as they can. Record the time in the box. Repeat the exercise.

Dictation

Grandpa __ __ __ __ __ __ to see

__ __ __ __ __ __ __ __ __ in Australia.

Nan __ __ __ __ __ at her __ __ __ __ __

because __ __ __ __ __ __ __ __ __ was rather far

away. They set off in the Fab Cab and landed in

__ __ __ __ __ __ __ __ __. They

__ __ __ __ __ __ their hats __ __ __ __ __

it __ __ __ very hot. Then they ate a picnic of

__ __ __ __ __ and __ __ __ __ __ __ __ __.

Grandpa fed the __ __ __ __ __ __ __ __ salad.

The __ __ __ __ __ __ __ __ __ hopped closer and

closer. Nan __ __ __ __ __ because she was

__ __ __ __ __ __. She bundled

__ __ __ __ __ __ __ into the Fab Cab and set off.

Grandpa w a n t e d to see w a ll a b ie s in Australia. Nan looked at her w a tch because Au s t r a l i a was rather far away. They set off in the Fab Cab and landed in Au s t r a l i a. They s w a pp ed their hats b e c au se it w a s very hot. Then they ate a picnic of s a l a d and s au s a g e s. Grandpa fed the w a ll a b ie s salad. The w a ll a b ie s hopped closer and closer. Nan c ou gh ed because she was n er v ou s. She bundled G r a n d p a into the Fab Cab and set off.

Use the text at the bottom of the page for dictation. Fold the page on the dotted line. Dictate the passage to the pupil. Ask her/him to spell the missing words, writing a sound on each line. Explain that a longer line indicates a spelling with more than one letter e.g. n igh t. Ask the pupil to unfold the sheet and check his/her spellings. This sheet may be photocopied by the purchaser.

Level 4 Book 3: 'Australia' <o> <a> <ou> <au>

Phonic patterns

Colour in the words with 'o' spellings

land	Austria	fast
long	orange	Australia
wash	out	watch
comedy	aunt	cough
sausage	want	touch

swan	
soup	
because	
ostrich	
wallaby	

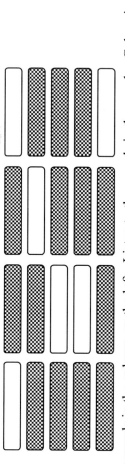

Fold this sheet on the dotted line. Read the words in the column on the left. Listen to the sounds in the words. Colour in the words that have 'o' spellings. Repeat this in the other columns. Unfold the sheet and check the correct words have been coloured in.

This sheet may be photocopied by the purchaser. © Phonic Books Ltd 2014

Reading game

<o> <a> <ou> <au>

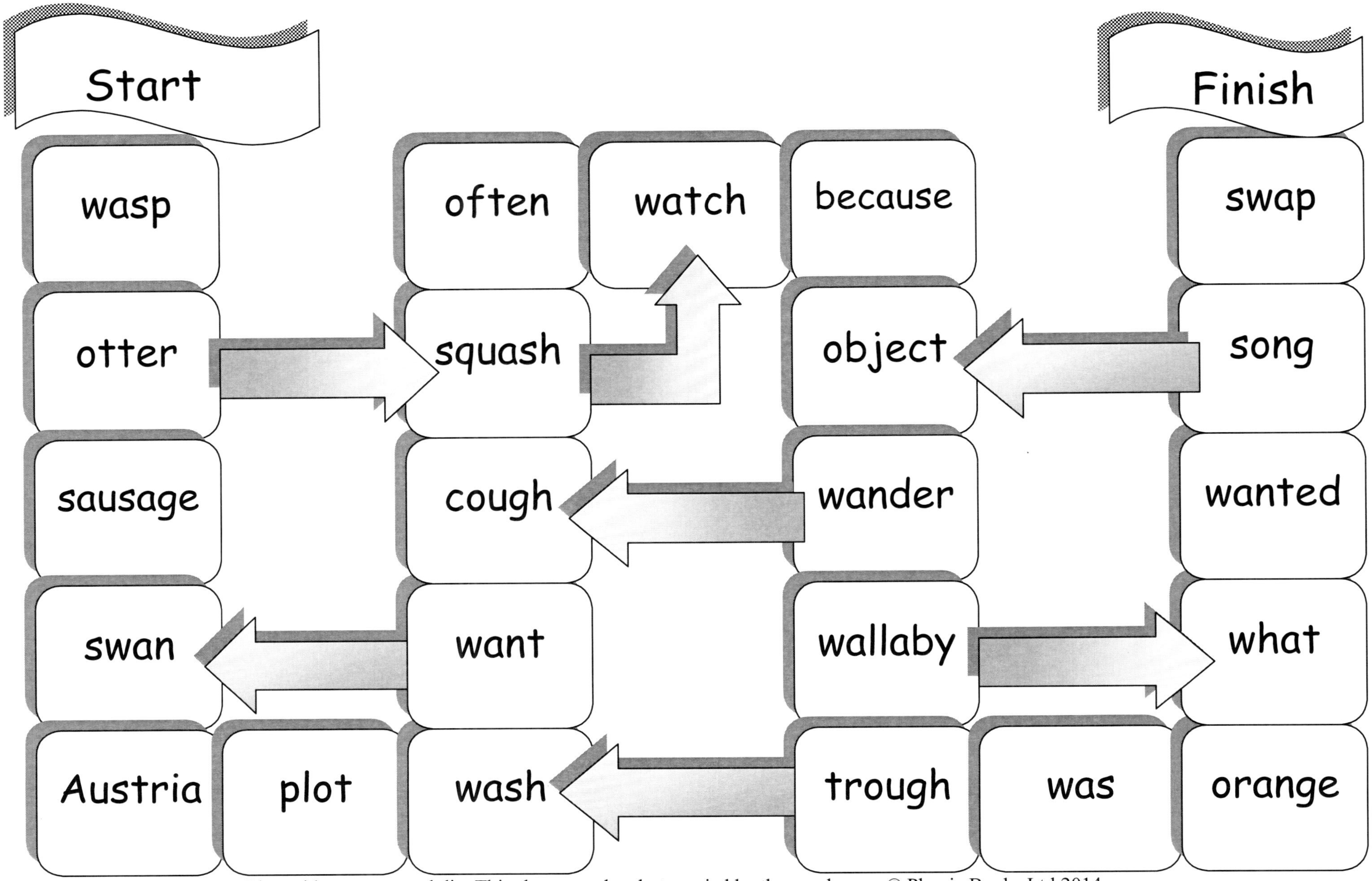
Start
wasp
otter
sausage
swan
Austria
plot
wash
want
cough
squash
often
watch
because
object
wander
wallaby
trough
was
orange
what
wanted
song
swap
Finish

Level 4 Book 3: 'Australia' <a> <o> <ou> <au>

Spelling assessment

1.

a	**o**	**ou**	**au**
want	blog	cough	because
was	strong	trough	sausage
what	dropped		Austria
watch	stopping		Australia

- -

2.

a
wash
watches
swallow
wasp
wander
squash

This list can be used as a spelling assessment at the end of each unit of work.
The teacher can add words from list 2 for able pupils. When dictating a word, say the word.
Then say a sentence with the word in it (to put the word in the context of a sentence) and then repeat
the word. E.g. "Tuesday. On Tuesday, we went on a school trip. Tuesday". This ensures that the
pupil has heard the word correctly. This sheet may be photocopied by the purchaser.

The Extended Phonic Code
Level 4 Book 4

'Five Excited Mice' – ‹s› ‹ss› ‹se› ‹st› ‹sc› ‹c› ‹ce›

Blending with 's' spellings   page 47

Reading practice   page 48

Reading and spelling   page 49

Chunking two-syllable words with 's' spellings   page 50

Reading comprehension – find the untruths*   page 51

Punctuation exercise – capital letters and full stops   page 52

Non-fiction reading and comprehension:
The mouse - true or false?   page 53

Write the story in your own words   page 54

Timed reading exercise   page 55

Dictation   page 56

Phonic patterns   page 57

Reading game   page 58

Spelling assessment: words with 's' spellings   page 59

*The untruths: Mother Mouse did not have nine mice; Cecil did not bounce on the trampoline; Jason did not crash into a wall; Tracy and Lucy did not cut up their dressing gowns.

Level 4 Book 4: 'Five Excited Mice'

<s> <ss> <se> <st> <sc> <c> <ce>

Blending with 's' spellings

s	o	ck	
d	r	e	ss	
n	i	ce	
c	y	c	le	
m	ou	se	
m	u	sc	le	
c	a	st	le	

Blend the sounds into words. Draw a picture in the box to match each word.

‹s› ‹ss› ‹se› ‹st› ‹sc› ‹c› ‹ce›

Reading practice

parcel	stress	classic
rinse	house	fence
muscle	glisten	scent
ceiling	pencil	science
jostle	circle	chase
face	wrestle	's' spellings ‹s› ‹ss› ‹se› ‹st› ‹sc› ‹c› ‹ce›

Level 4 Book 4: 'Five Excited Mice'

‹s› ‹ss› ‹se› ‹st› ‹sc› ‹c› ‹ce›

Reading and spelling

List the words according to the 's' spellings

s	ss	se	st
___	___	___	___
___	___	___	___
___	___	___	___
___	___	___	___
___	___	___	___
___	___	___	___

sc	c	ce
___	___	___
___	___	___
___	___	___
___	___	___
___	___	___
___	___	___

dress   stink   lace   spice   cycle   louse   scene   rustle   scissors
force   press   silent   cement   scent   loose   listen   parcel
whistle   sweep   bless   race   sense   muscle   wrestle   worse
chase   stain   pencil   fleece   gloss   castle   princess   chestnut
descend   cereal   voice   cross   minus   rinse

Level 4 Book 4: 'Five Excited Mice'

‹s› ‹ss› ‹se› ‹st› ‹sc› ‹c› ‹ce›

Chunking two-syllable words with 's' spellings

restful	rest	ful	restful
classic			
nicely			
city			
nonsense			
muscle			
listen			
cycle			
replace			
release			
science			
castle			
certain			
scissors			

Split the word into two syllables. Write each syllable in a box. Write the whole word while saying the syllables. This sheet may be photocopied by the purchaser. © Phonic Books Ltd 2014

Reading comprehension - find the untruths

Mother Mouse had nine baby mice. They were called Cedric, Lucy, Cecil, Jason and Tracy. Cecil bounced on the trampoline and hit his head on the ceiling. Cecil and Jason wrestled on the sofa and broke Mum's ceramic lamp. Jason raced downhill on his bicycle and crashed into a wall. Tracy and Lucy decided to make dresses for their dolls. They got the scissors and cut up their dressing gowns.

There are **4** untruths in the story above. Can you spot them?

Level 4 Book 4: 'Five Excited Mice'

<s> <ss> <se> <st> <sc> <c> <ce>

Punctuation exercise

Capital letters and full stops

tracy and lucy decided to make some dresses for their dolls they got the scissors and cut up the curtains mother mouse was so relieved when all five excited mice skipped off to school

There are **5** capital letters and **3** full stops missing.
Did you spot them all?

Ask the pupil to read through the text and add in capital letters and full stops where necessary. Encourage the pupil to read the text aloud as this will help him/her identify where the sentences stop.

This sheet may be photocopied by the purchaser. © Phonic Books Ltd 2014

Level 4 Book 4: 'Five Excited Mice'

<s> <ss> <se> <st> <sc> <c> <ce>

The mouse - true or false?

The mouse is a small mammal that belongs to the rodent family. Other examples of rodents are rats, squirrels, hamsters and guinea pigs. The mouse has a pointed snout; small, round ears and a long, hairless tail. The mouse is nocturnal. This means it is active at night. It has poor eyesight and a keen sense of hearing. It relies on its sense of smell to find food and avoid predators. The mouse has adapted to many different environments and is a very successful mammal. Baby mice are called pups. There can be 10-12 pups in a litter of baby mice.

A rodent is a kind of animal.

Mice have a hairy tail.

Mice have good eyesight.

Mice sleep at night.

A litter is a group of baby mice.

Ring the 'thumbs up' if the statement is true and the 'thumbs down' if it is not.

Level 4 Book 4: 'Five Excited Mice'

<s> <ss> <se> <st> <sc> <c> <ce

Write the story in your own words

In the beginning,

_____

_____

_____

_____

Then,

_____

_____

_____

_____

In the end,

_____

_____

_____

_____

Ask the pupil to retell the story orally before writing it.

Level 4 Book 4: 'Five Excited Mice'

<s> <ss> <se> <st> <sc> <c> <ce>

Timed reading exercise

mouse loose fancy sense ceiling city whistle listen parcel

pencil scene castle glance muscle purse rinse dressing

horse scissors wrestle fence dance December sauce

	1st try
Time:	

mouse loose fancy sense ceiling city whistle listen parcel

pencil scene castle glance muscle purse rinse dressing

horse scissors wrestle fence dance December sauce

	2nd try
Time:	

mouse loose fancy sense ceiling city whistle listen parcel

pencil scene castle glance muscle purse rinse dressing

horse scissors wrestle fence dance December sauce

	3rd try
Time:	

This timed reading exercise is for the pupil to improve his/her reading speed and fluency. Ask the pupil to read the words as fast as they can. Record the time in the box. Repeat the exercise.
This sheet may be photocopied by the purchaser. © Phonic Books Ltd 2014

Level 4 Book 4: 'Five Excited Mice'

<s> <ss> <se> <st> <sc> <c> <ce>

Dictation

Mother __ ____ ____ had five __ __ __ __ __ __ __ little __ __ ____. They were very naughty and never __ __ ____ __ __ ____ to her __ __ __ __ ____. Cedric __ ____ __ __ ____ on the sofa and hit the __ ____ __ __ ____. Cecil and Jason ____ __ ____ __ ____ and broke the ceramic lamp. Jason __ __ __ ____ downhill on his __ __ __ __ __ ____ and crashed into a __ __ __ ____. Tracy and Lucy __ __ __ __ __ __ __ to make __ __ __ ____ __ __ for their dolls. They got the ____ __ ____ ____ __ and cut up the __ ____ __ ____ __ __.

Mother M ou se had five e x c i t e d little m i ce. They were very naughty and never l i st e n ed to her a d v i ce. Cedric b ou n c ed on the sofa and hit the c ei l i ng. Cecil and Jason wr e st l ed and broke the ceramic lamp. Jason r a c ed downhill on his b i c y c le and crashed it into a f e n ce. Tracy and Lucy d e c i d e d to make d r e ss e s for their dolls. They got the sc i ss or s and cut up the c ur t ai n s.

Use the text at the bottom of the page for dictation. Write a sound on each line e.g.: c u te.
Remind the pupils that sound can be spelled by more than one letter.
A longer line indicates a spelling with more than one letter e.g. n igh t.

Level 4 Book 4: 'Five Excited Mice' <s> <ss> <se> <st> <sc> <c> <ce>

Phonic patterns

Colour in the words with 's' spellings

muscle	planet	scissors	clap
gossip	desk	dream	drink
lake	message	choice	space
centre	mountain	central	chase
balance	peace	twice	clown

Fold this sheet on the dotted line. Read the words in the column on the left. Listen to the sounds in the words. Colour in the words that have 's' spellings. Repeat this in the other columns. Unfold the sheet and check the correct words have been coloured in.
This sheet may be photocopied by the purchaser. © Phonic Books Ltd 2014

Level 4 Book 4: 'Five Excited Mice'

Reading game

⟨s⟩ ⟨ss⟩ ⟨se⟩ ⟨st⟩ ⟨sc⟩ ⟨c⟩ ⟨ce⟩

Start

Finish

place	dose	scent	castle	recent
ceiling	twice	purse	loss	rice
central	scissors	face	piece	stag
	sense		cycle	muscle
horse	circle	castle	listen	bliss

Play with counters and die. This sheet may be photocopied by the purchaser. © Phonic Books Ltd 2014

Spelling assessment

s	ss	ce	c
self	dress	face	circle
sad	class	place	cycle
risk	guess	nice	December
seen	press	twice	pencil

se	sc	st
house	science	listen
mouse	scent	whistle
horse	scene	castle
nonsense	scissors	chestnut

This list can be used as a spelling assessment at the end of each unit of work.
When dictating a word, say the word. Then say a sentence with the word in it (to put the word in the context of a sentence) and then repeat the word. E.g. "Tuesday. On Tuesday, we went on a school trip. Tuesday". This ensures that the pupil has heard the word correctly. The teacher can include homophones, e.g. 'seen/scene' but will need to explain them to the pupil.

The Extended Phonic Code
Level 4 Book 5

'Carrots and Celery' – <c>

Blending with the spelling <c>   page 61

Reading practice   page 62

Reading and spelling   page 63

Chunking multisyllable words with spelling <c>   page 64

Reading comprehension – find the untruths*   page 65

Punctuation exercise – capital letters and full stops   page 66

Non-fiction reading and comprehension:
Grow your own carrots – true or false?   page 67

Write the story in your own words   page 68

Timed reading exercise   page 69

Dictation   page 70

Phonic patterns   page 71

Reading game   page 72

Spelling assessment: words with spelling <c>   page 73

*The untruths: Pip and Pam did not sit down to eat breakfast; Pam did not love carrots and celery; Pip did not chop the carrots up into squares; Pip did not eat up all the vegetables.

Blending with the spelling <c>

c	y	c	le	

c	a	m	p	

c	ir	c	le	

c	a	k	e	

Blend the sounds into words. Draw a picture in the box to match each word.
<a-e> is presented on half squares as it is a split vowel digraph. © Phonic Books Ltd 2014

Reading practice

cycle	circus	parcel
circle	access	success
celery	cinema	decide
clown	cider	centre
century	catch	pencil
collide	city	Words with sounds 'k' and 's' for the spelling <c>

Reading and spelling

List the words according to the sound of the spelling <c>

<c> as 'k'	<c> as 's'
_____	_____
_____	_____
_____	_____
_____	_____
_____	_____
_____	_____
_____	_____
_____	_____
_____	_____
_____	_____
_____	_____

city   camp   December   circle   crab   cinema
clips   circus   pencil   cars   cement   carrots
castle   climb   cinnamon   celebrate   century
excite   crackle   certain   crisps   cleaner

Chunking multisyllabic words with the spelling <c>

carrots	carr	ots	carrots
circle			
success			
city			
certain			
centre			
cancel			
camel			
concert			
parcel			
celery				
December				
cinema				
celebrate				

Split the word into syllables. Write each syllable in a box. Write the whole word while saying the syllables. This sheet may be photocopied by the purchaser. © Phonic Books Ltd 2014

Reading comprehension - find the untruths

Pip and Pam sat down to eat breakfast. Pip offered Pam carrots and celery. Pam loved carrots and celery. Pam decided she wanted to eat cereal instead. Pip tried to get Pam to eat the vegetables. He chopped the carrots into squares. He made a centipede out of carrots and celery sticks. Then he got Pam to eat the carrots and celery by playing a game. In the end, Pip ate up the carrots and celery sticks.

There are **4** untruths in the story above. Can you spot them?

Punctuation exercise

Capital letters and full stops

pip and pam sat down to eat lunch pip
offered pam carrots and celery but
pam did not want to eat the vegetables
she wanted cereal instead pip got pam
to eat the vegetables by playing a game

There are **8** capital letters and **4** full stops missing.
Did you spot them all?

Ask the pupil to read through the text and add in capital letters and full stops where necessary.
Encourage the pupil to read the text aloud as this will help him/her identify where the sentences stop.
This sheet may be photocopied by the purchaser. © Phonic Books Ltd 2014

Non-fiction reading and comprehension:

Grow your own carrots - true or false?

Instructions: How to grow your own carrots

You will need: Carrot seeds, rake, fork, labels

Method:

1. Choose a sunny spot with light, sandy soil
2. Dig over the soil in winter
3. Take out any big stones and rake over
4. Sow the carrot seeds on a sunny day in March or April
5. Sow the seeds in drills 2-4 cm deep
6. Cover the soil and label each row
7. When a few leaves start to show, thin out the seedlings
8. Your carrots will be ready to eat in June or July
9. If the weather is dry and it doesn't rain, water the plants

drill – grooves in the soil
seedlings – baby plants
to thin out – pull out seedlings leaving one every 5cm

Carrots can grow in the dark.	👍	👎
Plant the seeds in the spring.	👍	👎
A drill is a groove in the soil.	👍	👎
Pick your carrots in the winter.	👍	👎
If the weather is wet, water the seedlings.	👍	👎

Ring the 'thumbs up' if the statement is true and the 'thumbs down' if it is not.

Write the story in your own words

In the beginning,

_____

_____

_____

_____

Then,

_____

_____

_____

_____

In the end,

_____

_____

_____

_____

Timed reading exercise

carrots   celery   ceiling   cycle   camping   call   contest   cereal

pencil   certain   concert   December   careful   cell   centre

cramp   celebrate   candle   camel   excited   princess   city

1st try
Time:

carrots   celery   ceiling   cycle   camping   call   contest   cereal

pencil   certain   concert   December   careful   cell   centre

cramp   celebrate   candle   camel   excited   princess   city

2nd try
Time:

carrots   celery   ceiling   cycle   camping   call   contest   cereal

pencil   certain   concert   December   careful   cell   centre

cramp   celebrate   candle   camel   excited   princess   city

3rd try
Time:

Dictation

Pip made __ __ ____ __ __ __ and

__ __ __ __ __ __ for lunch. Pam hated

__ __ __ __ __ __ __ __ __ __!

Pip ____ __ ____ ____ up the carrots into

__ ____ __ ____ __. He made the carrots look

like a __ __ __ __ __ __ __ __ ⌣ ___.

Pam said she wanted __ __ __ __ __ __ instead.

Pip asked Pam if she __ __ __ __ __ __ to play

a game. "__ ____ __ __ __ __ __ __" she said.

Pam had to eat the __ ____ __ __ __ __ __. Pam

played until all the __ __ __ __ __ __ and

__ __ __ __ __ __ sticks had been eaten!

Pip made c a rr o t s and c e l e r y for lunch. Pam hated
v e g e t a b le s! Pip ch o pp ed up the carrots into c ir c le s. He made
the carrots look like a c e n t i p e de. Pam said she wanted c e r e a l
instead. Pip asked Pam if she w a n t e d to play a game. "C er t ai n l y!"
she said. Pam had to eat the c ou n t er s. Pam played until all the
c a rr o t s and c e l e r y sticks had been eaten.

Use the text at the bottom of the page for dictation. Fold the page on the dotted line. Dictate the
passage to the pupil. Ask her/him to spell the missing words, writing a sound on each line. Explain
that a longer line indicates a spelling with more than one letter e.g. n igh t. Ask the pupil to unfold the
sheet and check his/her spellings. This sheet may be photocopied by the purchaser.

Level 4 Book 5: 'Carrots and Celery' <c>

Phonic patterns

Colour in only words with the spelling <c> that is pronounced 's'

contest	cylinder	cloud	city
cereal	cement	cream	recent
cramp	country	certain	ceiling
centre	celebrate	pencil	chase
cyber	princess	picnic	magic

Fold this sheet on the dotted line. Read the words in the column on the left. Listen to the sounds in the words. Colour in the lozenges with words that have the spelling <c> that is pronounced 's'. Repeat this in the other columns. Unfold the sheet and check the correct words have been coloured in.

This sheet may be photocopied by the purchaser. © Phonic Books Ltd 2014

Level 4 Book 5: 'Carrots and Celery'

Reading game   <c>

Start

clam	cycle	centre	cosy	ceiling
pencil	city		crown
central	circle	carrots	recent
celery	excite	cereal	careful	colour
				parcel

Finish

| concert | decide | castle | certain | cell |

Level 4 Book 5: 'Carrots and Celery' <c>

Spelling assessment

1.

c

circle

cycle

December

pencil

princess

2.

c

celebrate

centre

receive

cinema

excited

This list can be used as a spelling assessment at the end of each unit of work.
When dictating a word, say the word. Then say a sentence with the word in it (to put the word in the context of a sentence) and then repeat the word. E.g. "Tuesday. On Tuesday, we went on a school trip. Tuesday". This ensures that the pupil has heard the word correctly. List 2 can be offered to able pupils. This sheet may be photocopied by the purchaser. © Phonic Books Ltd 2014

The Extended Phonic Code
Level 4 Book 6

'The Camel' – ‹l› ‹ll› ‹el› ‹il› ‹al› ‹le› ‹ol›

Blending with 'l' spellings   page 75

Reading practice   page 76

Reading and spelling   page 77

Chunking multisyllable words with 'l' spellings   page 78

Reading comprehension – find the untruths*   page 79

Punctuation exercise – capital letters and full stops   page 80

Non-fiction reading and comprehension:
The camel – true or false?   page 81

Write the story in your own words   page 82

Timed reading exercise   page 83

Dictation   page 84

Phonic patterns   page 85

Reading game   page 86

Spelling assessment: words with 'l' spellings   page 87

*The untruths: It was not a rainy day; the camel did not stumble on the wet grass; Aunt March did not fall from the saddle; the camel did not nibble strawberries; Mr Basil did not tickle the camel.

‹l› ‹ll› ‹el› ‹il› ‹al› ‹le› ‹ol›

Blending with 'l' spellings

l	i	ck	

	w	a	ll	

c	a	m	el	

A	p	r	il	

m	e	d	al	

b	o	tt	le	

s	y	m	b	ol	

Blend the sounds into words. Draw a picture in the box to match each word.

‹l› ‹ll› ‹el› ‹il› ‹al› ‹le› ‹ol›

Reading practice

parcel	handle	pupil
pencil	medal	loft
drill	camel	symbol
animal	council	signal
mammal	sniffle	bubble
single	petrol	'l' spellings ‹l› ‹ll› ‹el› ‹il› ‹al› ‹le› ‹ol›

Photocopy this page onto card and cut into cards for reading practice.
The reader can sort the words according to the alternative spellings of the sound 'l'.
This sheet may be photocopied by the purchaser. © Phonic Books Ltd 2014

Level 4 Book 6: 'The Camel'

‹l› ‹ll› ‹el› ‹il› ‹al› ‹le› ‹ol›

Reading and spelling

List the words according to the 'l' spellings

l	ll	el	il
___	___	___	___
___	___	___	___
___	___	___	___
___	___	___	___
___	___	___	___
___	___	___	___

al	le	ol
___	___	___
___	___	___
___	___	___
___	___	___
___	___	___

camel petrol signal animal middle litter spell pencil
pupil model thrill sniffle trickle idol metal silly
limping travel symbol equal simple lentil council kennel
noodle mammal central cancel circle

<l> <ll> <el> <il> <al> <le> <ol>

Chunking multisyllable words with 'l' spellings

lucky	luck	y	lucky
calling			
cancel			
pencil			
metal			
eagle			
petrol			
smelly			
travel			
council			
mammal			
noodle			
symbol			
animal			

Split the word into two syllables. Write each syllable in a box. Write the whole word while saying the syllables. This sheet may be photocopied by the purchaser. © Phonic Books Ltd 2014

Reading comprehension - find the untruths

One rainy day in April, Aunt March put a saddle on her camel. She gave a signal for the camel to bend down. Aunt March clambered on. The camel stumbled on the wet grass. Aunt March fell from the saddle. When they got to the vegetable market, the camel galloped over to nibble the strawberries. Then Mr Basil tickled the camel under his chin. Aunt March finally got the camel back to the castle by feeding him apples all the way home.

There are 5 untruths in the story above. Can you spot them?

Punctuation exercise

Capital letters and full stops

aunt march climbed up onto the saddle
she sat on the camel the camel
stumbled on the pebble stones aunt
march nearly toppled from the saddle
the camel nibbled the carrots

There are **7** capital letters and **5** full stops missing.
Did you spot them all?

Level 4 Book 6: 'l'

<l> <ll> <el> <il> <al> <le> <ol>

Non-fiction reading and comprehension
The camel - true or false?

> The word **'adapted'** here means that camels have developed qualities that are suitable for living in a hot desert.

There are two kinds of camels in the world today: the one-humped camel and the two-humped camel. Both kinds have been domesticated (do-mes-ti-ca-ted) which means tamed to live alongside humans. They are used for their milk, meat and their hair. They are also used to transport humans and to carry heavy loads. Camels have even been used like horses for soldiers to ride in battle. They live 40-50 years. Camels are very well adapted to hot climates. They can go without water for a long time. People used to think that they store water in their humps but, actually, they store fat in their humps.

There are three kinds of camel in the world.   👍   👎

'Domesticated' means living alongside humans.   👍   👎

Camels are very useful animals.   👍   👎

Camels live in cold climates.   👍   👎

The camel's hump stores fat, not water.   👍   👎

Ring the 'thumbs up' if the statement is true and the 'thumbs down' if it is not.

Write the story in your own words

In the beginning,

_____

_____

_____

_____

Then,

_____

_____

_____

_____

In the end,

_____

_____

_____

_____

Timed reading exercise

camel small evil pupil pedal cancel pencil jungle circle

idol medal double little petrol Bristol poodle gravel

central council nostril travel candle tunnel fossil cycle

1st try	
Time:	

camel small evil pupil pedal cancel pencil jungle circle

idol medal double little petrol Bristol poodle gravel

central council nostril travel candle tunnel fossil cycle

2nd try	
Time:	

camel small evil pupil pedal cancel pencil jungle circle

idol medal double little petrol Bristol poodle gravel

central council nostril travel candle tunnel fossil cycle

3rd try	
Time:	

Dictation

Aunt March gave a __ __ __ __ ____ and the

__ __ __ ____ bent down. She climbed on

and sat in the __ __ ____ ____. The camel

__ __ __ __ __ __ ____ on the

__ __ ____ ____ stones. Then it saw the

__ __ __ __ __ __ and ran over to it. It

__ __ __ __ __ ____ up a lettuce and

__ __ __ __ __ ____ on the carrots.

Mr __ __ __ ____ was not __ __ ____ __ ____!

He __ __ __ __ __ __ __ ____ and said the camel

was a rude __ __ __ __ ____!

Aunt March gave a s i g n al and the c a m el bent down. She climbed on
and sat in the s a dd le. The camel s t u m b l ed on the p e bb le stones.
Then it saw the m ar k e t and ran over to it. It g o bb l ed up a lettuce
and n i bb l ed on the c a rr o t s. Mr B a s il was not p l ea s ed!
He g r u m b l ed and said the camel was a rude a n i m al!

Use the text at the bottom of the page for dictation. Fold the page on the dotted line. Dictate the
passage to the pupil. Ask her/him to spell the missing words, writing a sound on each line. Explain
that a longer line indicates a spelling with more than one letter e.g. n igh t. Ask the pupil to unfold the
sheet and check his/her spellings. This sheet may be photocopied by the purchaser.

Level 4 Book 6: 'The Camel' <l> <ll> <el> <il> <al> <le> <ol>

Phonic patterns

Colour in the words with 'l' spellings

muscle	stumble	nesting	circle
panel	idol	funnel	dressed
crisps	pedal	cancel	metal
lentil	travel	central	handle
rubbish	racket	blister	petrol

Fold this sheet on the dotted line. Read the words in the column on the left. Listen to the sounds in the words. Colour in the lozenges with words that have 'l' spellings. Repeat this in the other columns. Unfold the sheet and check the correct words have been coloured in.

This sheet may be photocopied by the purchaser. © Phonic Books Ltd 2014

Reading game

<l> <ll> <el> <il> <al> <le> <ol>

Start

Finish

letter	yellow	central	pistol	lollipop
lentil	cancel		symbol	evil
ballet	circle	cycle		pupil
pencil	travel	able		petrol
idol	medal	atlas	beetle	plural	kennel

Spelling assessment

l	**ll**	**el**	**il**
like	small	label	pencil
lots	called	model	April
live	all	camel	pupil
let's	I'll	travel	evil

al	**le**	**ol**
medal	little	idol
animal	middle	symbol
mammal	table	petrol
final	circle	pistol

This list can be used as a spelling assessment at the end of each unit of work.
When dictating a word, say the word. Then say a sentence with the word in it (to put the word in the context of a sentence) and then repeat the word. E.g. "Tuesday. On Tuesday, we went on a school trip. Tuesday". This ensures that the pupil has heard the word correctly. The teacher can include homophones, e.g. 'new/knew' but will need to explain them to the pupil.

The Extended Phonic Code
Level 4 Book 7

'The Ginger Cat' – ‹j› ‹g› ‹ge› ‹dge›

Blending with 'j' spellings   page 89

Reading practice   page 90

Reading and spelling   page 91

Chunking multisyllable words with 'j' spellings   page 92

Reading comprehension – find the untruths*   page 93

Punctuation exercise – capital letters and full stops   page 94

Non-fiction reading and comprehension: Cats – true or false?   page 95

Write the story in your own words   page 96

Timed reading exercise   page 97

Dictation   page 98

Phonic patterns   page 99

Reading game   page 100

Spelling assessment: words with 'j' spellings   page 101

*The untruths: Shep was not a legend because he was big; Tosh did not have big, sharp teeth; Shep and Tosh did not see a giraffe; Shep and Tosh did not cross the bridge.

Blending with 'j' spellings

| j | u | g | |

| g | e | m | |

| l | ar | ge | |

| b | r | i | dge | |

Blend the sounds into words. Draw a picture in the box to match each word.
© Phonic Books Ltd 2014

Reading practice

hedge	nudge	ginger
gerbil	jacket	damage
cottage	village	gym
badge	pledge	magic
luggage	junk	germ
major	giraffe	'j' spellings <j> <g> <ge> <dge>

Photocopy this page onto card and cut into cards for reading practice.
The reader can sort the words according to the alternative spellings of the sound 'j'.
This sheet may be photocopied by the purchaser. © Phonic Books Ltd 2014

Reading and spelling

List the words according to the 'j' spellings

j	g
_____	_____
_____	_____
_____	_____
_____	_____
_____	_____

ge	dge
_____	_____
_____	_____
_____	_____
_____	_____
_____	_____

justice   gentle   judge   hedge   jar   magic
village   garage   large   gerbil   ginger   digital
damage   Japan   digest   bridge   jacket   dodge
cottage   manage   sledge   smudge

Chunking multisyllable words with 'j' spellings

junkyard	junk	yard	junkyard
magic			
cartridge			
manage			
legend			
cottage			
gerbil			
judgement			
gentle			
energy				
genius				
village			
giraffe			
joking			

Split the word into syllables. Write each syllable in a box. Write the whole word while saying the syllables. This sheet may be photocopied by the purchaser. © Phonic Books Ltd 2014

Reading comprehension - find the untruths

Shep, the dog, was a legend because he was very big. He won a badge for being the gentlest dog. Tosh was not gentle. The other dogs just kept out of his way. They dodged him because he had big, sharp teeth. One day, Shep and Tosh saw a giraffe on a bridge. The ginger cat looked savage. Tosh growled but the cat did not budge. Shep and Tosh managed to cross the bridge.

There are **4** untruths in the story above. Can you spot them?

Punctuation exercise

Capital letters and full stops

shep was huge and gentle tosh was
little and fierce tosh scared the big
dogs away they met a savage ginger cat
on a bridge the cat hissed and flashed
its fangs the dogs hid behind the hedge

There are **6** capital letters and **6** full stops missing.
Did you spot them all?

Non-fiction reading and comprehension
Cats - true or false?

Vocabulary
originate – where something comes from
domesticated - tamed and kept as a pet or on a farm
flexible – able to bend
retractable – able to draw back
vision - sight

Cats are amazing animals! Common cats originate from the African wildcat. They belong to the feline family of smaller wild cats including cheetahs. They were domesticated by humans about 10,000 years ago. Cats were worshipped in ancient Egypt. Cats have flexible bodies and retractable (re-trac-tab-le) claws. They have sharp teeth for killing small prey. Cats can see in the dark and can hear sounds that humans cannot hear like the sounds that mice make. They don't have good colour vision but they have a very good sense of smell.

Common cats came from the wildcat in Africa. 👍 👎

Common cats are related to cheetahs. 👍 👎

Cats can pull their claws back into their paws. 👍 👎

Cats can't see in the dark. 👍 👎

Humans can hear better than cats. 👍 👎

Cats have a good sense of smell. 👍 👎

Ring the 'thumbs up' if the statement is true and the 'thumbs down' if it is not.

Write the story in your own words

In the beginning,

_____

_____

_____

_____

Then,

_____

_____

_____

_____

In the end,

_____

_____

_____

_____

Ask the pupil to retell the story orally before writing it.

Timed reading exercise

jelly jumble gerbil large bridge lodge major giant magic

cottage badge gentle jacket hedge fudge ginger logic

page age sledge fridge damage gym tragic giraffe

1st try
Time:

jelly jumble gerbil large bridge lodge major giant magic

cottage badge gentle jacket hedge fudge ginger logic

page age sledge fridge damage gym tragic giraffe

2nd try
Time:

jelly jumble gerbil large bridge lodge major giant magic

cottage badge gentle jacket hedge fudge ginger logic

page age sledge fridge damage gym tragic giraffe

3rd try
Time:

This timed reading exercise is for the pupil to improve his/her reading speed and fluency. Ask the pupil to read the words as fast as they can. Record the time in the box. Repeat the exercise.

Dictation

Shep was a __ __ ____ dog. He was a

__ __ __ __ ___ __ __ __ __ __! In the park,

he was a __ __ __ __ __ __! He won a

__ __ _____ for the gentlest dog! Tosh was

little and fierce. He __ __ __ __ __ ____ to

__ __ _____ the big dogs away. They had to

__ __ _____ his ____ ____ __ little teeth.

One day, Shep and Tosh went for a __ ____ __

on a __ __ __ _____. A huge

__ __ __ __ ____ cat sat in the middle of it.

Tosh growled but it would not __ __ _____.

Shep was h̲ u̲ ge̲ dog. He was a g̲ e̲ n̲ t̲ le̲ g̲ i̲ a̲ n̲ t̲. In the park, he was a l̲ e̲ g̲ e̲ n̲ d̲! He won a b̲ a̲ dge̲ for the gentlest dog! Tosh was little and fierce. He m̲ a̲ n̲ a̲ g̲ ed̲ to s̲ c̲ are̲ the big dogs away. They had to d̲ o̲ dge̲ his sh̲ ar̲ p̲ little teeth. One day, Shep and Tosh went for a w̲ al̲ k̲ on a b̲ r̲ i̲ dge̲. A huge g̲ i̲ n̲ g̲ er̲ cat sat in the middle of it. Tosh growled but it would not b̲ u̲ dge̲.

Use the text at the bottom of the page for dictation. Fold the page on the dotted line. Dictate the passage to the pupil. Ask her/him to spell the missing words, writing a sound on each line. Explain that a longer line indicates a spelling with more than one letter e.g. n̲ igh̲ t̲. Ask the pupil to unfold the sheet and check his/her spellings. This sheet may be photocopied by the purchaser.

Level 4 Book 7: 'The Ginger Cat' ‹j› ‹g› ‹ge› ‹dge›

Phonic patterns

Colour in the words with 'j' spellings

snatch	ginger	bridge	grandad
great	plank	legend	register
gentle	grumble	gladly	flower
badge	giant	engine	smudge
dungeon	glitter	pledge	gym

Fold this sheet on the dotted line. Read the words in the column on the left. Listen to the sounds in the words. Colour in the words that have 'j' spellings. Repeat this in the other columns. Unfold the sheet and check the correct words have been coloured in.

This sheet may be photocopied by the purchaser. © Phonic Books Ltd 2014

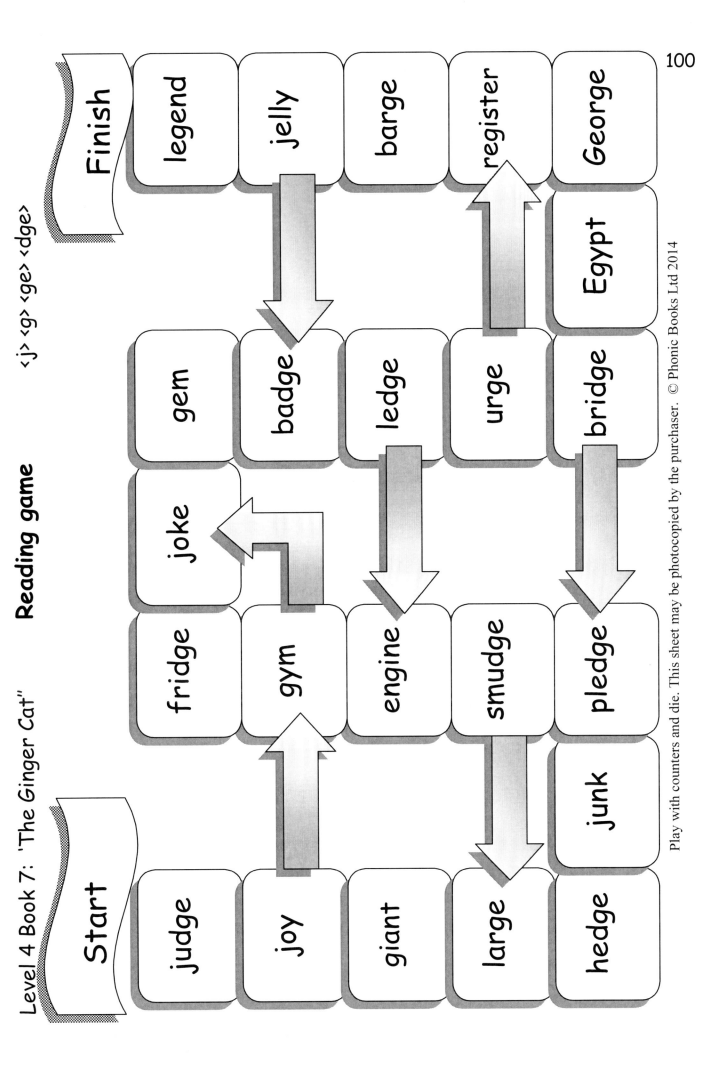

Start

judge

joy

giant

large

hedge

junk

fridge

gym

engine

smudge

pledge

joke

gem

badge

ledge

urge

bridge

Egypt

Finish

legend

jelly

barge

register

George

Spelling assessment

j	**g**	<u>**ge**</u>	<u>**dge**</u>
June	magic	village	edge
July	giant	cottage	bridge
just	ginger	courage	hedge
jump	giraffe	large	badge

This list can be used as a spelling assessment at the end of each unit of work.
When dictating a word, say the word. Then say a sentence with the word in it (to put the word in the context of a sentence) and then repeat the word. E.g. "Tuesday. On Tuesday, we went on a school trip. Tuesday". This ensures that the pupil has heard the word correctly. This sheet may be photocopied by the purchaser. © Phonic Books Ltd 2014

The Extended Phonic Code
Level 4 Book 8

'George' – ‹g›

Blending with the spelling ‹g›   page 103

Reading practice   page 104

Reading and spelling   page 105

Chunking multisyllable words with spelling ‹g›   page 106

Reading comprehension – find the untruths*   page 107

Punctuation exercise – capital letters and full stops   page 108

Non-fiction reading and comprehension:
How to care for your gerbils - true or false?   page 109

Write the story in your own words   page 110

Timed reading exercise   page 111

Dictation   page 112

Phonic patterns   page 113

Reading game   page 114

Spelling assessment: words with the spelling ‹g›   page 115

*The untruths: Grandpa's door was not yellow; he didn't plant sunflowers in the pots; he didn't fetch straw for the fire; his cup of tea didn't disappear; he didn't hide behind the giant chair.

Blending with the spelling \<g\>

g	oo	se	

g	er	b	il	

g	e	m	

g	a	t	e	

Blend the sounds into words. Draw a picture in the box to match each word.
\<a-e\> is presented on half squares as it is a split vowel digraph. © Phonic Books Ltd 2014

Reading practice

giant	grand	gym
germ	gentle	grind
gone	ginger	digital
magic	grass	legend
gem	gladly	rigid
giraffe	games	Words with the sounds 'g' and 'j' for the spelling <g>

Reading and spelling

List the words according to the sound of the spelling ‹g›

‹g› as 'g'	‹g› as 'j'
_____	_____
_____	_____
_____	_____
_____	_____
_____	_____
_____	_____
_____	_____
_____	_____
_____	_____
_____	_____
_____	_____

gerbil grandad George gate gravel
great gym gentle glad magic logic register
grapes giant group gasp ginger good grab
giraffe glitter grammar germ genius

Chunking multisyllable words with the spelling <g>

grandad	*gran*	*dad*	*grandad*
gentle			
magic			
gerbil			
gladly			
legend			
giant			
engine			
gravel			
giraffe			
gymnastics			
generous			
register			
digital			

Split the word into syllables. Write each syllable in a box. Write the whole word while saying the syllables. This sheet may be photocopied by the purchaser. © Phonic Books Ltd 2014

Reading comprehension - find the untruths

Grandpa lived in a pretty, little cottage. In the spring, he painted the door yellow. He planted sunflowers in the pots. One night, just when Grandpa had nestled down with his tea and ginger biscuits, the fire went out. He went to fetch some straw for the fire. When he got back, his cup of tea had disappeared! Just like magic! He set a trap for the thief. He hid behind the giant chair and waited.

There are **5** untruths in the story above. Can you spot them?

Punctuation exercise

Capital letters and full stops

grandpa decided to catch the thief he hid behind the giant grandfather clock and waited the little thief appeared it was a gerbil grandpa called him george and made him a gym

There are **6** capital letters and **5** full stops missing.
Did you spot them all?

Non-fiction reading and comprehension
How to care for your gerbils - true or false?

How to care for your gerbils

1. Get more than one gerbil as they are social animals and are not used to living alone.
2. Get gerbils from the same family as gerbils from different families will fight.
3. Get gerbils of the same sex otherwise they will soon have babies.
4. Get a tank for them with soil so they can burrow tunnels like they do in the wild.
5. Make sure they have a water bottle in the tank and check it always has water in it.
6. Feed your gerbils healthy meals including vegetables.
7. Do not feed your gerbils potatoes, rhubarb or tomato leaves as they are poisonous for them.
8. Make sure your gerbil has some fun and exercise.
9. Handle your gerbils regularly so that they are tame.

Keep only one gerbil.	👍	👎
Don't get a boy and a girl gerbil.	👍	👎
Gerbils like to swim in the tank.	👍	👎
Gerbils do not need to drink water.	👍	👎
Gerbils need exercise to keep healthy.	👍	👎

Ring the 'thumbs up' if the statement is true and the 'thumbs down' if it is not.

Write the story in your own words

In the beginning,

_____

_____

_____

_____

Then,

_____

_____

_____

_____

In the end,

_____

_____

_____

_____

Timed reading exercise

gerbil giant grand goggles gentle glitter magic gym

ginger globe gladly glare tragic giraffe gist general

grass greater logic gate gem register glisten engine

1st try
Time:

gerbil giant grand goggles gentle glitter magic gym

ginger globe gladly glare tragic giraffe gist general

grass greater logic gate gem register glisten engine

2nd try
Time:

gerbil giant grand goggles gentle glitter magic gym

ginger globe gladly glare tragic giraffe gist general

grass greater logic gate gem register glisten engine

3rd try
Time:

This timed reading exercise is for the pupil to improve his/her reading speed and fluency. Ask the pupil to read the words as fast as they can. Record the time in the box. Repeat the exercise.

Dictation

Grandpa went to __ __ _____ logs for the
fire. When he got back, his __ __ __ __ ____
biscuits had __ __ __ __ ____ _____ ____.
Just like __ __ __ __ __! He decided to
__ __ _____ the ____ ____ __. He hid
__ __ __ __ __ __ the __ __ __ __ __ clock.
Soon a little __ ____ __ ____ appeared.
__ __ __ __ __ __ __ called him George.
____ ____ ____ had lots of __ __ ____ __ __
so Grandpa made him a __ __ ____ ____
__ __ __.

- -

Grandpa went to f e tch logs for the fire. When he got back, his
g i n g er biscuits had d i s a pp ear ed. Just like m a g i c! He decided
to c a tch the th ie f. He hid b e h i n d the g i a n t clock. Soon a
little g er b il appeared. G r a n d p a called him George. Ge or ge had
lots of e n er g y so Grandpa made him a l i tt le g y m.

Use the text at the bottom of the page for dictation. Fold the page on the dotted line. Dictate the
passage to the pupil. Ask her/him to spell the missing words, writing a sound on each line. Explain
that a longer line indicates a spelling with more than one letter e.g. n igh t. Ask the pupil to unfold the
sheet and check his/her spellings. This sheet may be photocopied by the purchaser.

Level 4 Book 8: 'George' <g>

Phonic patterns

Colour in <u>only</u> words with the spelling <g> pronounced 'j'

magical	ginger	glisten	general
giant	goat	gerbil	register
gentle	grumble	gladly	granny
garden	legend	engine	germ
glaring	glitter	greater	gym

Fold this sheet on the dotted line. Read the words in the column on the left. Listen to the sounds in the words. Colour in the words that have the spelling <g> that is pronounced 'j'. Repeat this in the other columns. Unfold the sheet and check the correct words have been coloured in. This sheet may be photocopied by the purchaser. © Phonic Books Ltd 2014

Reading game   <g>

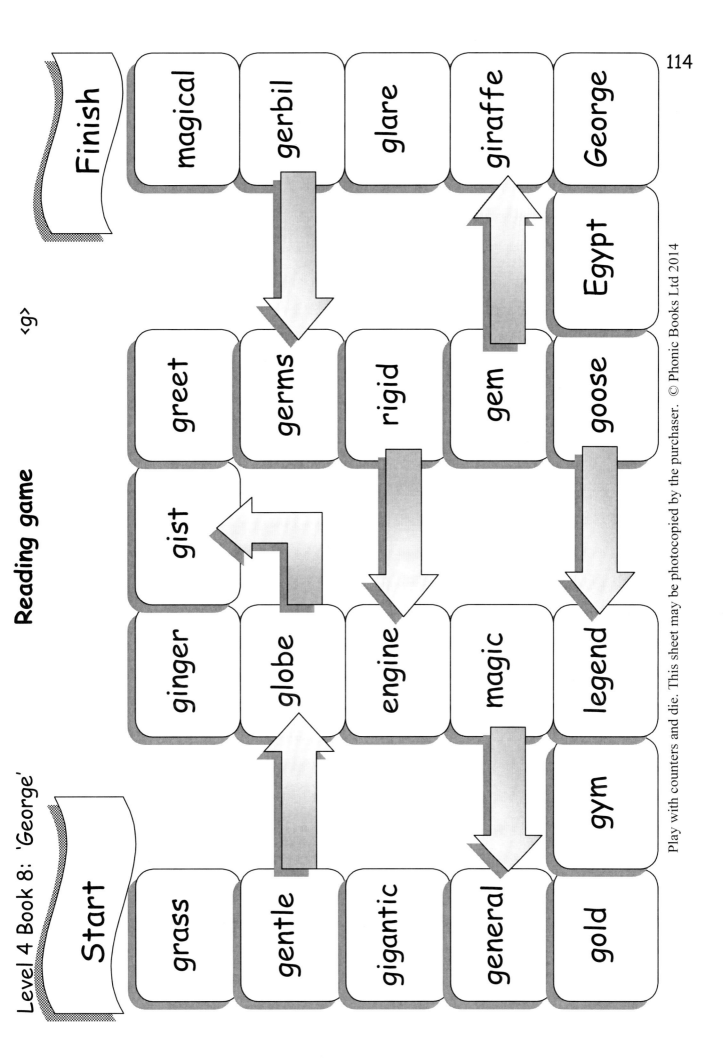

Start

Finish

grass	ginger	magical
gentle	globe	gerbil
gigantic	engine	germs
	rigid	glare
general	magic	gem
		giraffe
gold	gym	legend
	goose	Egypt
		George

Level 4 Book 8: 'George' <g>

Spelling assessment

1.

```
g

great

giant

gentle

magic

legend
```

2.

```
g

gym

germ

digital

gigantic

giraffe
```

This list can be used as a spelling assessment at the end of each unit of work.
When dictating a word, say the word. Then say a sentence with the word in it (to put the word in the context of a sentence) and then repeat the word. E.g. "Tuesday. On Tuesday, we went on a school trip. Tuesday". This ensures that the pupil has heard the word correctly. List 2 can be offered to able pupils. This sheet may be photocopied by the purchaser. © Phonic Books Ltd 2014

The Extended Phonic Code
Level 4 Book 9

'Steph, the Elephant' – ‹f› ‹ff› ‹ph› ‹gh›

Blending with 'f' spellings   page 117

Reading practice   page 118

Reading and spelling   page 119

Chunking multisyllable words with 'f' spellings   page 120

Reading comprehension – find the untruths*   page 121

Punctuation exercise – capital letters and full stops   page 122

Non-fiction reading and comprehension:
Elephants – true or false?   page 123

Write the story in your own words   page 124

Timed reading exercise   page 125

Dictation   page 126

Phonic patterns   page 127

Reading game   page 128

Spelling assessment: words with 'f' spellings   page 129

*The untruths: Aunt March did not get Steph from a farm; Aunt March did not play the flute to cheer Steph up; Phil was not a beekeeper; the elephants did not push Aunt March into the moat.

Blending with 'f' spellings

f	i	sh	

c	l	i	ff	

ph	o	t	o	

l	au	gh	

Blend the sounds into words. Draw a picture in the box to match each word.

Reading practice

trophy	ferry	coffee
cough	photo	dolphin
famous	offend	offer
sphere	prophet	orphan
effect	graph	enough
rough	draught	'f' spellings ‹f› ‹ff› ‹ph› ‹gh›

Reading and spelling

List the words according to the 'f' spellings

f	ff
_____	_____
_____	_____
_____	_____
_____	_____
_____	_____

ph	gh
_____	_____
_____	_____
_____	_____
_____	_____
_____	_____

dolphin   cough   fig   stuff   saxophone   orphan
frame   cliff   enough   laughed   draughts   rough
tough   prophet   sphere   alphabet   offend
suffer   buffalo   fragment   coffee   frail

Chunking multisyllable words with 'f' spellings

friendly	friend	ly	friendly
photo			
laughing			
dolphin			
trophy			
coughing			
enough			
orphan			
roughly			
elephant			
alphabet			
megaphone			
physical			
atmosphere			

Split the word into syllables. Write each syllable in a box. Write the whole word while saying the syllables. This sheet may be photocopied by the purchaser. © Phonic Books Ltd 2014

Reading comprehension - find the untruths

Steph, the elephant, was an orphan. Aunt March got her from the farm. Steph was unhappy. Aunt March could see she was having a rough time. Aunt March played the flute to cheer her up. Steph just looked offended. Aunt March phoned Phil, the beekeeper. He suggested that Steph missed her sister, Daphne. In the end, Daphne came to stay. The elephants pushed Aunt March into the moat.

There are **4** untruths in the story above. Can you spot them?

Punctuation exercise

Capital letters and full stops

steph, the elephant, was an orphan she was very sad aunt march tried to cheer her up by playing the saxophone aunt march called phil, the zookeeper he told her that steph missed her sister

There are **9** capital letters and **5** full stops missing.
Did you spot them all?

Ask the pupil to read through the text and add in capital letters and full stops where necessary.
Encourage the pupil to read the text aloud as this will help him/her identify where the sentences stop.

Non-fiction reading and comprehension
Elephants - true or false?

Elephants are the biggest land animals on earth. They are related to mammoths which are now extinct. There are two kinds of elephants. The African elephant is larger and has bigger ears. The Asian elephant is smaller. Female elephants live in groups. At the centre of the group are the calves (babies). They are looked after by their mother and their aunties. Elephants are considered very intelligent animals. Scientists believe they are able to understand the feelings of other elephants. Some elephants are endangered because poachers kill them for their ivory tusks.

mammoths – lived on earth until 45,000 years ago. They looked like huge elephants with very big tusks.
poachers – people who hunt illegally
endangered – at risk of becoming extinct
ivory – the white material that tusks are made from.

Elephants are the largest animals on earth.	👍	👎
There is only one kind of elephant.	👍	👎
The Asian elephant has bigger ears.	👍	👎
Elephant calves are looked after by their dad.	👍	👎
Some elephants are endangered.	👍	👎
Poachers hunt elephants for their tusks.	👍	👎

Ring the 'thumbs up' if the statement is true and the 'thumbs down' if it is not.

Write the story in your own words

In the beginning,

_____

_____

_____

_____

Then,

_____

_____

_____

_____

In the end,

_____

_____

_____

_____

Timed reading exercise

dolphin phone cough laugh sphere graph elephant aphid

trophy orphan autograph phantom physical prophet tough

rough toffee enough draughts effect suffer photo

| 1st try |
| Time: |

dolphin phone cough laugh sphere graph elephant aphid

trophy orphan autograph phantom physical prophet tough

rough toffee enough draughts effect suffer photo

| 2nd try |
| Time: |

dolphin phone cough laugh sphere graph elephant aphid

trophy orphan autograph phantom physical prophet tough

rough toffee enough draughts effect suffer photo

| 3rd try |
| Time: |

Dictation

Steph, the __ __ __ ___ __ __ __, was an orphan. She came to ___ __ __ March's castle from the zoo. __ __ __ ___ was very __ __ __ __ ___ __. Aunt March could see she was having a __ ___ ___ time. Aunt March tried to play the __ __ __ __ ___ __ ___. Then she ___ __ __ ___ Phil, the zookeeper. "Steph is an ___ ___ __ __ ," he explained. "She misses her sister, __ __ ___ __ __". When Daphne came to stay, they squirted Aunt March with __ __ __ ___.

Steph, the e l e ph a n t, was an orphan. She came to Au n t March's castle from the zoo. S t e ph was very u n h a pp y. Aunt March could see she was having a r ou gh time. Aunt March tried to play the s a x o ph o ne. Then she ph o n ed Phil, the zookeeper. "Steph is an or ph a n," he explained. "She misses her sister, D a ph n e". When Daphne came to stay, they squirted Aunt March with w a t er.

Use the text at the bottom of the page for dictation. Fold the page on the dotted line. Dictate the passage to the pupil. Ask her/him to spell the missing words, writing a sound on each line. Explain that a longer line indicates a spelling with more than one letter e.g. n igh t. Ask the pupil to unfold the sheet and check his/her spellings. This sheet may be photocopied by the purchaser.

Level 4 Book 9: 'Steph, the Elephant' <f> <ff> <ph> <gh>

Phonic patterns

Colour in the words with 'f' spellings

photo	prank	pamphlet	flexible
graph	philosopher	prison	orphan
laughter	ghost	phrase	roughly
pyjamas	cough	prickly	planet
fantasy	guest	elephant	ghastly

Fold this sheet on the dotted line. Read the words in the column on the left. Listen to the sounds in the words. Colour in the lozenges with words that have 'f' spellings. Repeat this in the other columns. Unfold the sheet and check the correct words have been coloured in.

This sheet may be photocopied by the purchaser. © Phonic Books Ltd 2014

Level 4 Book 9: 'Steph, the Elephant'   **Reading game**   <f> <ff> <ph> <gh>

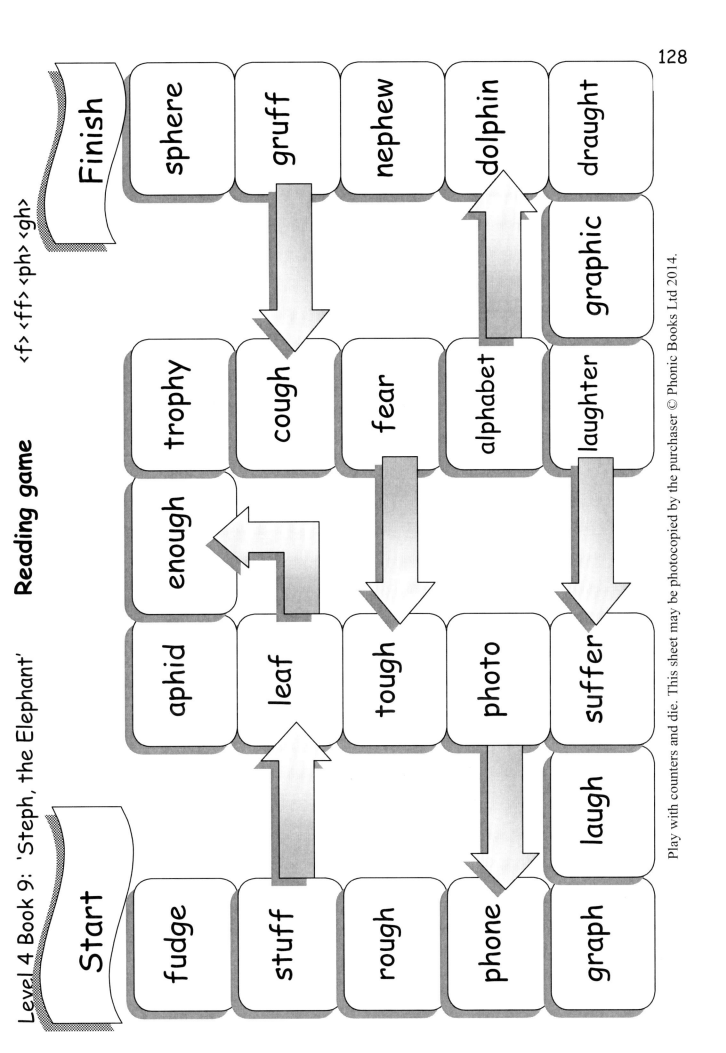

Play with counters and die. This sheet may be photocopied by the purchaser © Phonic Books Ltd 2014.

Spelling assessment

f	**ff**	**ph**	**gh**
fast	stuff	phone	laughed
find	different	photo	cough
before	suffer	nephew	tough
friends	offend	elephant	enough
		orphan	
		sphere	
		graph	

This list can be used as a spelling assessment at the end of each unit of work.
When dictating a word, say the word. Then say a sentence with the word in it (to put the word in the
context of a sentence) and then repeat the word. E.g. "Tuesday. On Tuesday, we went on a school
trip. Tuesday". This ensures that the pupil has heard the word correctly.

The Extended Phonic Code
Level 4 Book 10

'A Grand Adventure' – suffix ‹-ture›

Blending with the suffix ‹-ture›   page 131

Reading practice   page 132

Chunking multisyllable words with the suffix ‹-ture›   page 133

Reading comprehension – find the untruths*   page 134

Punctuation exercise – capital letters and full stops   page 135

New vocabulary   page 136

Write the story in your own words   page 137

Timed reading exercise   page 138

Dictation   page 139

Phonic patterns   page 140

Reading game   page 141

Spelling assessment: words with the suffix ‹-ture›   page 142

*The untruths: Rex did not set off in the evening; he did not slip out of the door; Rex did not go on the slide.

Blending with the suffix <-ture>

n	a	ture	

m	i	x	ture	

p	i	c	ture	

c	a	p	ture	

Blend the sounds and suffixes into words. Draw a picture in the box to match each word.
© Phonic Books Ltd 2014

Reading practice

mixture	future	creature
adventure	culture	departure
furniture	capture	feature
posture	lecture	structure
puncture	gesture	picture
nature	rupture	Words with the suffix <-ture>

Chunking multisyllable words with the suffix <-ture>

nature	na	ture	nature
future			
creature			
picture			
feature			
lecture			
capture			
mixture			
culture			
structure			
puncture			
departure			
furniture			
adventure			

Split the word into syllables. Write each syllable in a box. Write the whole word while saying the syllables. This sheet may be photocopied by the purchaser. © Phonic Books Ltd 2014

Reading comprehension - find the untruths

Rex sat next to the window and longed for an adventure in nature. The next evening, when it was dark, he left a note on the table and set off. He slipped out of the door. At last, his adventure had begun! All of a sudden, a creature grabbed him and whisked him off his feet. He had been captured! The creature made him go on the slide. Then Liz found him and brought him home.

There are **3** untruths in the story above. Can you spot them?

Punctuation exercise

Capital letters and full stops

rex sat at the window and looked out he wanted to see nature he resolved to go on a grand adventure he left a note on the table he slipped out of the window and slid down a rope

There are **5** capital letters and **5** full stops missing.
Did you spot them all?

New vocabulary

capture – to take control by force

lecture – a long talk given to an audience or a telling off

departure – the act of leaving

gesture – a movement of head or body expressing an idea

structure - a building or something built from smaller parts

manufacture – make something using machinery

- -

We must not miss the time of _____.

The children climbed up the _____.

The soldiers will _____ the city.

The man made a _____ with his hand.

The professor gave a long, boring _____.

They _____ the boots in a factory.

Read and explain the new words to the pupils. Give an example of how the word is used in a sentence. Ask the pupil to explain the word. The pupil then writes the correct word in the sentences below. Reread the sentences to check they make sense.

Write the story in your own words

In the beginning,

_____

_____

_____

_____

Then,

_____

_____

_____

_____

In the end,

_____

_____

_____

_____

Timed reading exercise

adventure nature capture picture lecture future culture

mixture gesture feature creature puncture structure

departure agriculture

1st try
Time:

adventure nature capture picture lecture future culture

mixture gesture feature creature puncture structure

departure agriculture

2nd try
Time:

adventure nature capture picture lecture future culture

mixture gesture feature creature puncture structure

departure agriculture

3rd try
Time:

Dictation

Rex __ __ __ __ __ __ to go on a grand
__ __ __ __ __ _____. He longed to see
__ __ _____! One __ ____ __ __ ____, he
left a note and a __ __ __ _____ of himself
on the kitchen table. He __ __ __ __ ____ ____
what the __ __ _____ would hold for him.
He climbed up on the __ ____ __ __ _____,
slipped out of the __ __ __ __ ____ and slid
down a rope. Soon a __ __ ____ _____
picked him up. Rex was __ __ __ _____d!

Rex w a n t e d to go on a grand a d v e n ture. He longed to see
n a ture! One m or n i ng, he left a note and a p i c ture of himself on
the kitchen table. He w o n d er ed what the f u ture would hold for
him. He climbed up on the f ur n i ture, slipped out of the w i n d ow
and slid down a rope. Soon a c r ea ture picked him up. Rex was
c a p ture d!

Use the text at the bottom of the page for dictation. Fold the page on the dotted line. Dictate the
passage to the pupil. Ask her/him to spell the missing words, writing a sound on each line. Explain
that a longer line indicates a spelling with more than one letter e.g. n igh t. Ask the pupil to unfold the
sheet and check his/her spellings. This sheet may be photocopied by the purchaser.

Phonic patterns

Colour in the words with the suffix <-ture>

future	creature	dragon	fracture
graph	temple	puncture	expenditure
vulture	furniture	fixture	kitten
nature	culture	lecture	agriculture
plastic	hundreds	elephant	feature

Fold this sheet on the dotted line. Read the words in the column on the left. Listen to the sounds in the words. Colour in the lozenges with words that have the suffix <-ture>. Repeat this in the other columns. Unfold the sheet and check the correct words have been coloured in.

This sheet may be photocopied by the purchaser. © Phonic Books Ltd 2014

Level 4 Book 10: 'A Grand Adventure'   **Reading game**   suffix <-ture>

Finish

| literature | vulture | miniature | denture | signature |

| | | | | caricature |

| fixture | creature | feature | lecture | texture |

| puncture | furniture | departure | gesture | mixture |

| | | | | culture |

Start

| nature | picture | capture | adventure | future |

| structure |

Play with counters and die. This sheet may be photocopied by the purchaser © Phonic Books Ltd 2014.

Spelling assessment

‹-ture›

picture

mixture

adventure

creature

capture

structure

nature

This list can be used as a spelling assessment at the end of each unit of work.
When dictating a word, say the word. Then say a sentence with the word in it (to put the word in the context of a sentence) and then repeat the word. E.g. "Tuesday. On Tuesday, we went on a school trip. Tuesday". This ensures that the pupil has heard the word correctly.

The Extended Phonic Code
Level 4 Book 11

'The Inspection' – suffix <-tion>

Blending with the suffix <-tion>   page 145

Reading practice   page 146

Chunking multisyllable words with the suffix <-tion>   page 147

Reading comprehension – find the untruths*   page 148

Punctuation exercise – capital letters and full stops   page 149

New vocabulary   page 150

Write the story in your own words   page 151

Timed reading exercise   page 152

Dictation   page 153

Phonic patterns   page 154

Reading game   page 155

Spelling assessment: words with the suffix <-tion>   page 156

*The untruths: Viv's room was not tidy; Mum did not say the inspection would be in the evening; they didn't pretend the toys would have an examination; the toys didn't line up at the bus station.

Blending with the suffix <-tion>

n	a	tion	

s	t	a	tion	

p	o	tion	

a	dd	i	tion	

Blend the sounds and suffixes into words. Draw a picture in the box to match each word.

Reading practice

competition	invention	potion
nation	creation	affection
action	addition	fraction
intention	station	collection
infection	mention	portion
fiction	inspection	Words with the suffix <-tion>

Chunking multisyllable words
with the suffix <-tion>

nation	na	tion	nation
fiction			
action			
mention			
station			
lotion			
fraction			
ration			
potion			
invention			
connection			
collection			
attention			
addition			

Split the word into syllables. Write each syllable in a box. Write the whole word while saying the syllables. This sheet may be photocopied by the purchaser. © Phonic Books Ltd 2014

Reading comprehension - find the untruths

Viv's room was very tidy. Mum got fed up and announced that there would be an inspection that evening. Viv had good intentions but then Fred came to play. He came with his action hero toy. They pretended that the toys had to have an examination. The toys were lined up at the bus station. Viv forgot all about the inspection and went to bed. In the night, the toys got into action and tidied up her room.

There are **4** untruths in the story above. Can you spot them?

Punctuation exercise

Capital letters and full stops

fred came to play with his action hero
viv and fred pretended the toys were
going on a vacation they lined up all the
toys by the train station viv forgot
about the inspection of her room

There are **5** capital letters and **4** full stops missing.
Did you spot them all?

New vocabulary

portion – part of a whole, e.g. a portion of a pie

inspection – checking something carefully

intention – something that you plan to do

mention – to say something briefly

fiction - something that is made up and not true

caption – a label under a picture, photo or cartoon

The officer made an _____ of the tents.

I wrote a _____ under the photograph.

I cut the cake into _____s.

Despite the mess, she had good _____s.

Please don't _____ this to Dad.

I prefer reading _____.

Read and explain the new words to the pupils. Give an example of how the word is used in a sentence. Ask the pupil to explain the word. The pupil then writes the correct word in the sentences below. Reread the sentences to check they make sense.

Write the story in your own words

In the beginning,

_____

_____

_____

_____

Then,

_____

_____

_____

_____

In the end,

_____

_____

_____

_____

Timed reading exercise

station action invention reaction pollution fraction addition

subtraction edition nation collection mention portion

fiction option inspection suction construction

1st try

Time:

station action invention reaction pollution fraction addition

subtraction edition nation collection mention portion

fiction option inspection suction construction

2nd try

Time:

station action invention reaction pollution fraction addition

subtraction edition nation collection mention portion

fiction option inspection suction construction

3rd try

Time:

This timed reading exercise is for the pupil to improve his/her reading speed and fluency. Ask the pupil to read the words as fast as they can. Record the time in the box. Repeat the exercise.

Dictation

Viv's room was messy. Mum got fed up. She
__ ____ ____ __ __ ____ that there would be
an __ __ __ __ __ __ _____. Viv had good
__ __ __ __ __ _____ __ but then Fred
came to play. He __ __ _____ __ his
__ __ _____ hero. They pretended that the
toys were going on a __ __ __ __ _____.
The toys had to line up at the train
__ __ __ _____. In the night, the toys got
into __ __ _____ and tidied up the room.

Viv's room was messy. Mum got fed up. She a̲ nn o̲u̲ n c e̲d̲ that there
would be an i̲ n s p e c tion. Viv had good i̲ n t e̲ n tion s but then Fred
came to play. He b̲ r̲ ough t̲ his a̲ c tion hero. They pretended that the
toys were going on a v̲ a̲ c a̲ tion. The toys had to line up at the train
s̲ t̲ a̲ tion. In the night, the toys got into a̲ c tion and tidied up the
room.

Use the text at the bottom of the page for dictation. Fold the page on the dotted line. Dictate the
passage to the pupil. Ask her/him to spell the missing words, writing a sound on each line. Explain
that a longer line indicates a spelling with more than one letter e.g. n̲ igh t̲. Ask the pupil to unfold the
sheet and check his/her spellings. This sheet may be photocopied by the purchaser.
© Phonic Books Ltd 2014

Level 4 Book 11: 'The Inspection' suffix <-tion>

Phonic patterns

Colour in the words with the suffix <-tion>

station	creature	mixture	caption
nature	future	fraction	fiction
solution	portion	collection	kitten
relation	mention	lecture	section
action	invention	reaction	repetition

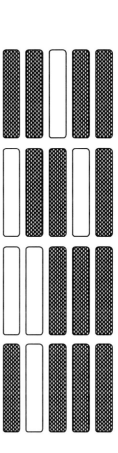

Fold this sheet on the dotted line.   Read the words in the column on the left.   Listen to the sounds in the words.   Colour in the lozenges with words that have the suffix <-tion>.   Repeat this in the other columns.   Unfold the sheet and check the correct words have been coloured in.

This sheet may be photocopied by the purchaser.   © Phonic Books Ltd 2014

Level 4 Book 11: 'The Inspection'

Reading game

suffix <-tion>

Start

Finish

action		lotion
nation	solution	evolution
relation	fraction	petition
collection	invention	function
mention	inspection	option
	reaction	potion
deletion		
addition		
repetition		
digestion		
station	instruction	
section		

Play with counters and die. This sheet may be photocopied by the purchaser. © Phonic Books Ltd 2014

Spelling assessment

<-tion>

nation

station

information

addition

subtraction

competition

invention

education

This list can be used as a spelling assessment at the end of each unit of work.
When dictating a word, say the word. Then say a sentence with the word in it (to put the word in the context of a sentence) and then repeat the word. E.g. "Tuesday. On Tuesday, we went on a school trip. Tuesday". This ensures that the pupil has heard the word correctly.
This sheet may be photocopied by the purchaser. © Phonic Books Ltd 2014

The Extended Phonic Code
Level 4 Book 12

'Viv's Profession' – suffixes <-ssion> and <-cian>

Blending with the suffix <-ssion>   page 159

Blending with the suffix <-cian>   page 160

Reading practice   page 161

Chunking multisyllable words with the suffixes <-ssion> and <-cian> page 162

Reading comprehension – find the untruths*   page 163

Punctuation exercise – capital letters and full stops   page 164

New vocabulary   page 165

Write the story in your own words   page 166

Timed reading exercise   page 167

Dictation   page 168

Phonic patterns   page 169

Reading game   page 170

Spelling assessment: words with the suffixes <-ssion> and <-cian>   page 171

*The untruths: Viv did not have a discussion with her brother; Mum did not have a passion for carrots; Grandpa did not have a passion for animals.

Blending and segmenting words with the suffix <-ssion>

mission	m	i	ssion			
passion						
impression						
profession						
permission						
possession						
discussion						
percussion						
aggression						
expression						

Blend the sounds and suffixes into words.   © Phonic Books Ltd 2014

Blending and segmenting words with the suffix <-cian>

optician	o	p	t	i	cian
magician					
musician					
technician						
beautician					
physician					

Reading practice

session	magician	permission
discussion	passion	mission
profession	optician	technician
possession	intermission	confession
compassion	physician	expression
impression	aggression	Words with the suffixes <-ssion> and <-cian>

Chunking multisyllable words
with the suffixes <-ssion> <-cian>

passion	pa	ssion	passion
mission			
session			
discussion				
permission				
possession				
admission				
profession				
impression				
musician				
physician				
optician				
technician				
magician				

Split the word into syllables. Write each syllable in a box. Write the whole word while saying the
syllables. This sheet may be photocopied by the purchaser. © Phonic Books Ltd 2014

Reading comprehension - find the untruths

Viv wanted to know what her profession would be when she grew up. She decided to have a discussion with her brother about it. First, she went to Mum. Mum told her that she had a passion for carrots and that is why she became a florist. Dad said he had a passion for robots so he became an electrician. Grandpa said he had a passion for animals and that is why he became a musician.

There are **3** untruths in the story above. Can you spot them?

Punctuation exercise

Capital letters and full stops

viv had a mission she wanted to know what she would be when she grew up she went to have a discussion with the adults in her family she decided that she had a passion for animals and dressing up

There are **4** capital letters and **4** full stops missing.

Did you spot them all?

Ask the pupil to read through the text and add in capital letters and full stops where necessary.
Encourage the pupil to read the text aloud as this will help him/her identify where the sentences stop.
This sheet may be photocopied by the purchaser. © Phonic Books Ltd 2014

New vocabulary

profession – a job someone does to earn money

possession – something that is owned

permission – allowing someone to do something

passion – a love for something or someone

musician – a person who plays a musical instrument

optician – a person who checks your eyes

My mum is a doctor. That is her _____.

I had to ask the teacher for her _____.

The _____s played in a rock band.

The _____ said I needed glasses.

I have a _____ for football.

My favourite _____ is my old teddy bear.

Read and explain the new words to the pupils. Give an example of how the word is used in a
sentence. Ask the pupil to explain the word. The pupil then writes the correct word in the sentences
below. Reread the sentences to check they make sense.

Write the story in your own words

In the beginning,

_____

_____

_____

_____

Then,

_____

_____

_____

_____

In the end,

_____

_____

_____

_____

Timed reading exercise

discussion profession magician musician passion mission

impression politician possession session technician

permission electrician depression beautician

1st try	
Time:	

discussion profession magician musician passion mission

impression politician possession session technician

permission electrician depression beautician

2nd try	
Time:	

discussion profession magician musician passion mission

impression politician possession session technician

permission electrician depression beautician

3rd try	
Time:	

This timed reading exercise is for the pupil to improve his/her reading speed and fluency. Ask the pupil to read the words as fast as they can. Record the time in the box. Repeat the exercise.

Dictation

Viv had a ___ ___ _____. She wanted to have

a ___ ___ ___ ___ ___ _____ with the adults

about their ___ ___ ___ ___ ___ _____s. Mum

had a ___ ___ _____ for flowers and became

a florist. Dad had a ___ ___ _____ for robots

and became an ___ ___ ___ ___ ___ ___ ___ _____.

Grandpa had a ___ ___ _____ for music and

became a ___ ___ ___ ___ _____. Viv had a

___ ___ _____ for animals and dressing up.

She would be a ___ ___ ___ ___ _____!

Viv had a <u>m</u> <u>i</u> <u>ssion</u>. She wanted to have a <u>d</u> <u>i</u> <u>s</u> <u>c</u> <u>u</u> <u>ssion</u> with the adults about their <u>p</u> <u>r</u> <u>o</u> <u>f</u> <u>e</u> <u>ssion</u> s. Mum had a <u>p</u> <u>a</u> <u>ssion</u> for flowers and became a florist. Dad had a <u>p</u> <u>a</u> <u>ssion</u> for robots and became an <u>e</u> <u>l</u> <u>e</u> <u>c</u> <u>t</u> <u>r</u> <u>i</u> <u>cian</u>. Grandpa had a <u>p</u> <u>a</u> <u>ssion</u> for music and became a <u>m</u> <u>u</u> <u>s</u> <u>i</u> <u>cian</u>. Viv had a <u>p</u> <u>a</u> <u>ssion</u> for animals and dressing up. She would be a <u>m</u> <u>a</u> <u>g</u> <u>i</u> <u>cian</u>!

Use the text at the bottom of the page for dictation. Fold the page on the dotted line. Dictate the passage to the pupil. Ask her/him to spell the missing words, writing a sound on each line. Explain that a longer line indicates a spelling with more than one letter e.g. <u>n</u> <u>igh</u> <u>t</u>. Ask the pupil to unfold the sheet and check his/her spellings. This sheet may be photocopied by the purchaser.

Level 4 Book 12: 'Viv's Profession' suffixes <-ssion> <-cian>

Phonic patterns

Colour in the words with the suffixes <-ssion> and <-cian>

profession	electrician	possession	beautician
mission	optician	technician	structure
capture	lecture	fixture	intermission
admission	permission	adventure	discussion
magician	picture	impression	politician

Fold this sheet on the dotted line. Read the words in the column on the left. Listen to the sounds in the words. Colour in the words that have the suffixes <-ssion> and <-cian>. Repeat this in the other columns. Unfold the sheet and check the correct words have been coloured in. Colour in the lozenges with words that have

This sheet may be photocopied by the purchaser. © Phonic Books Ltd 2014

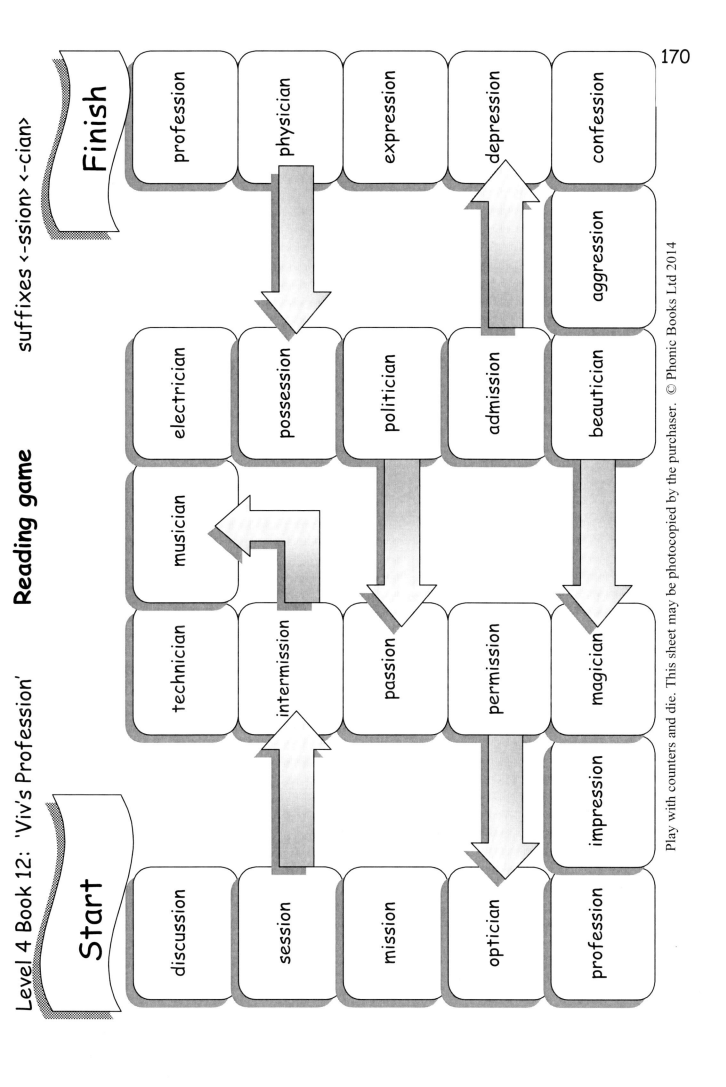

Level 4 Book 12: 'Viv's Profession'

Reading game

suffixes <-ssion> <-cian>

170

Start

Finish

discussion · session · mission · optician · profession

technician · intermission · passion · permission · magician · impression

musician

electrician · possession · politician · admission · beautician

profession · physician · expression · depression · confession · aggression

Play with counters and die. This sheet may be photocopied by the purchaser. © Phonic Books Ltd 2014

Spelling assessment

<-ssion>	**<-cian>**
passion	musician
mission	magician
permission	optician
discussion	electrician
expression	politician
impression	
possession	

This list can be used as a spelling assessment at the end of each unit of work.
When dictating a word, say the word. Then say a sentence with the word in it (to put the word in the context of a sentence) and then repeat the word. E.g. "Tuesday. On Tuesday, we went on a school trip. Tuesday". This ensures that the pupil has heard the word correctly.

The Extended Phonic Code
Level 4 Book 13

'The Treasure Hunt' – suffix <-sure>

Blending with the suffix <-sure>   page 173

Reading practice   page 174

Chunking multisyllable words with the suffix <-sure>   page 175

Reading comprehension – find the untruths*   page 176

Punctuation exercise – capital letters and full stops   page 177

New vocabulary   page 178

Write the story in your own words   page 179

Timed reading exercise   page 180

Dictation   page 181

Phonic patterns   page 182

Reading game   page 183

Spelling assessment: words with the suffix <-sure>   page 184

*The untruths: Mum did not make the treasure hunt; Alf did not find the first clue under a bush; Alf did not find a metal box; the key was not for a treasure chest.

Blending and segmenting words
with the suffix <-sure>

leisure	l	ei	sure		
treasure					
measure					
pleasure					
closure					
exposure					
composure					
enclosure					

Reading practice

leisure	treasure	measure
pleasure	exposure	composure
enclosure	displeasure	Words with the suffix ‹-sure›

Chunking multisyllable words
with the suffix <-sure>

leisure	lei	sure	leisure
measure			
treasure			
pleasure			
exposure			
composure			
enclosure			
displeasure			

Split the word into syllables. Write each syllable in a box. Write the whole word while saying the syllables. This sheet may be photocopied by the purchaser. © Phonic Books Ltd 2014

Reading comprehension - find the untruths

It was Alf's birthday. Mum made a treasure hunt for him in the garden. Alf loved treasure hunts. He walked about the garden leisurely. He found the first clue under a bush. It said "Take five strides to the left." He measured five strides to the left. Next, he found a clue by a flower pot. He took six strides forward. There he found a metal box. In the box was a key to a treasure chest.

There are **4** untruths in the story above. Can you spot them?

Punctuation exercise

Capital letters and full stops

it was alf's birthday and his dad made a treasure hunt for him alf had to follow the clues to find the treasure he found a key in a wooden box with the key to the shed inside it in the shed was a brand new bicycle

There are **5** capital letters and **4** full stops missing.
Did you spot them all?

New vocabulary

leisure – time when one is not working, free time

pleasure – a feeling of enjoyment

enclosure – an area that is surrounded by a fence

displeasure – a feeling of annoyance or disapproval

composure – feeling calm and in control of oneself

treasure – something very valuable like precious stones

- -

I kept my _____ before the exam.

It is a _____ to go to lie on the beach.

The man showed _____ by scowling.

In my _____ time I play the guitar.

The deer jumped over the _____.

The pirate hid the _____ in a cave.

Read and explain the new words to the pupils. Give an example of how the word is used in a sentence. Ask the pupil to explain the word. The pupil then writes the correct word in the sentences below. Reread the sentences to check they make sense.

Write the story in your own words

In the beginning,

_____

_____

_____

_____

Then,

_____

_____

_____

_____

In the end,

_____

_____

_____

_____

Ask the pupil to retell the story orally before writing it.

Timed reading exercise

treasure leisure measure pleasure displeasure enclosure

composure exposure treasure measure pleasure

1st try
Time:

treasure leisure measure pleasure displeasure enclosure

composure exposure treasure measure pleasure

2nd try
Time:

treasure leisure measure pleasure displeasure enclosure

composure exposure treasure measure pleasure

3rd try
Time:

This timed reading exercise is for the pupil to improve his/her reading speed and fluency. Ask the pupil to read the words as fast as they can. Record the time in the box. Repeat the exercise.

Dictation

It was Alf's birthday and Dad made a

__ __ ____ _____ hunt for him in the

garden. Alf had to __ __ ____ ____ the clues

to find the __ __ ____ _____. He walked

__ ____ _____ __ __ around the garden

looking for __ __ ____ __. The first clue was

tucked __ __ __ ____ a stone. Alf had to

__ ____ _____ five strides to the next clue.

His face lit up with __ __ ____ _____ when

he found the __ __ ____ _____.

It was Alf's birthday and Dad made a t r ea sure hunt for him in the
garden. Alf had to f o ll ow the clues to find the t r ea sure. He walked
l ei sure l y around the garden looking for c l ue s. The first clue was
tucked u n d er a stone. Alf had to m ea sure five strides to the next
clue. His face lit up with p l ea sure when he found the t r ea sure.

Use the text at the bottom of the page for dictation. Fold the page on the dotted line. Dictate the
passage to the pupil. Ask her/him to spell the missing words, writing a sound on each line. Explain
that a longer line indicates a spelling with more than one letter e.g. n igh t. Ask the pupil to unfold the
sheet and check his/her spellings. This sheet may be photocopied by the purchaser.
© Phonic Books Ltd 2014

Level 4 Book 13: 'The Treasure Hunt' suffix <-sure>

Phonic patterns

Colour in the words with the suffix <-sure>

potion	mission	reason	nation
exposure	mixture	leisure	treasure
enclosure	dipleasure	reflection	inspection
passion	composure	measure	session
station	rations	fiction	pleasure

Fold this sheet on the dotted line. Read the words in the column on the left. Listen to the sounds in the words. Colour in the lozenges with words that have the suffix <-sure>. Repeat this in the other columns. Unfold the sheet and check the correct words have been coloured in.

This sheet may be photocopied by the purchaser. © Phonic Books Ltd 2014

183

Level 4 Book 13: 'The Treasure Hunt'   **Reading game**   suffix <-sure>

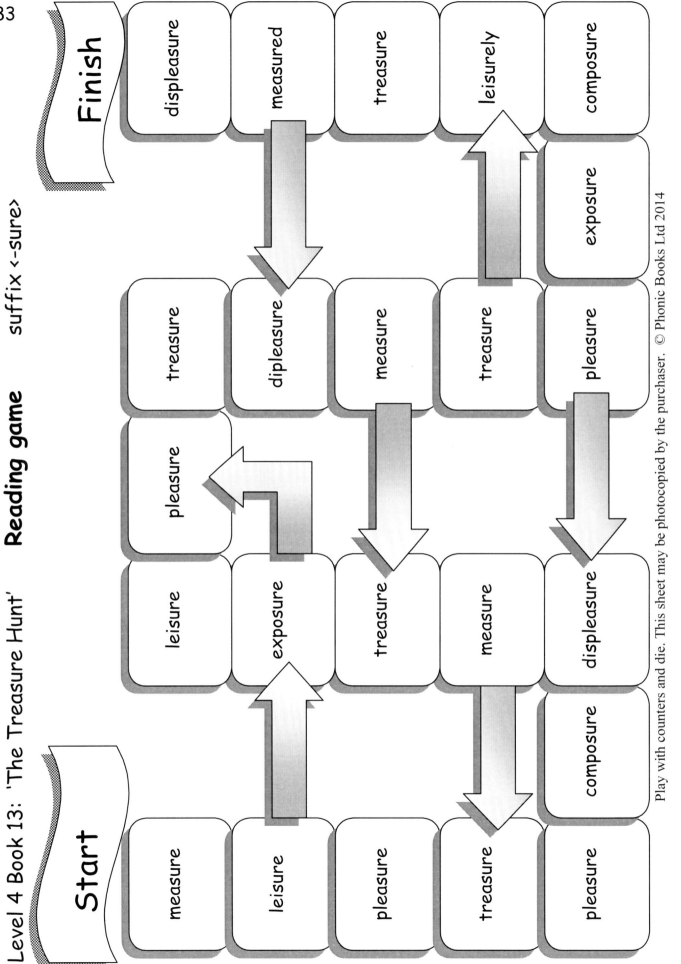

Start

Finish

measure · leisure · pleasure · treasure · pleasure

treasure · diplpeasure · measure · treasure · pleasure

leisure · exposure · treasure · measure · displeasure

pleasure

displeasure · measured · treasure · leisurely · composure

exposure · composure

Spelling assessment

‹**-sure**›

treasure

measure

pleasure

displeasure

leisure

This list can be used as a spelling assessment at the end of each unit of work.
When dictating a word, say the word. Then say a sentence with the word in it (to put the word in the context of a sentence) and then repeat the word. E.g. "Tuesday. On Tuesday, we went on a school trip. Tuesday". This ensures that the pupil has heard the word correctly.

The Extended Phonic Code
Level 4 Book 14

'Alien Invasion' – suffix <-sion>

Blending with the suffix <-sion>   page 187

Reading practice   page 188

Chunking multisyllable words with the suffix <-sion>   page 189

Reading comprehension – find the untruths*   page 190

Punctuation exercise – capital letters and full stops   page 191

New vocabulary   page 192

Write the story in your own words   page 193

Timed reading exercise   page 194

Dictation   page 195

Phonic patterns   page 196

Reading game   page 197

Spelling assessment: words with the suffix <-sion>   page 198

Blank reading game sheet   page 199

* The untruths: The children did not watch Spider Invasion; Grandpa did not say they could watch more television; Viv did not decide to dress up as a fairy; Grandpa did not make alien sandwiches.

Blending and segmenting words
with the suffix <-sion>

vision	v	i	sion		
division					
confusion					
decision					
invasion					
collision					
explosion					
occasion					
revision					

Reading practice

vision	division	confusion
revision	decision	collision
explosion	invasion	occasion

Words with the suffix <-sion>

Chunking multisyllable words
with the suffixes <-sion>

Word	Syllable 1	Syllable 2	Whole word
vision	vi	sion	vision
occasion			
confusion			
decision			
revision			
explosion			
collision			
division			
invasion			

Split the word into syllables. Write each syllable in a box. Write the whole word while saying the syllables. This sheet may be photocopied by the purchaser. © Phonic Books Ltd 2014

Reading comprehension - find the untruths

Sam and Jack came to visit Viv. They watched Spider Invasion on the television. Then Grandpa said that because it was a special occasion, they could watch more television. Viv made a decision to dress up as a fairy. Jack put on an alien suit and they played 'Alien Invasion'. There were collisions and explosions. Then little Sam got in the way and fell over. Grandpa made some alien sandwiches.

There are **4** untruths in the story above. Can you spot them?

Punctuation exercise

Capital letters and full stops

jack and sam came to visit viv they watched 'alien invasion', viv's favourite programme then viv dressed up as an astronaut and jack dressed up as an alien there were lots of explosions and collisions it was fun until sam fell over

There are **13** capital letters and **5** full stops missing.
Did you spot them all?

Ask the pupil to read through the text and add in capital letters and full stops where necessary.
Encourage the pupil to read the text aloud as this will help him/her identify where the sentences stop.

New vocabulary

invasion – when people take over someone else's country

occasion – a special event

confusion – when things get muddled up

collision – when things bump into each other violently

vision – the ability to see or imagine something

decision – making up your mind

The car did not stop and there was a _____.

The old, blind man had lost his _____.

I made a big _____ and quit playing soccer.

The Norman _____ happened in 1066.

In the _____, we forgot the dog.

I put on a clean shirt for the _____.

Read and explain the new words to the pupils. Give an example of how the word is used in a sentence. Ask the pupil to explain the word. The pupil then writes the correct word in the sentences below. Reread the sentences to check they make sense.

Write the story in your own words

In the beginning,

_____

_____

_____

_____

Then,

_____

_____

_____

_____

In the end,

_____

_____

_____

_____

Timed reading exercise

invasion explosion infusion confusion vision evasion

decision revision occasion persuasion collision division

provision erosion vision exclusion inclusion

1st try

Time:

invasion explosion infusion confusion vision evasion

decision revision occasion persuasion collision division

provision erosion vision exclusion inclusion

2nd try

Time:

invasion explosion infusion confusion vision evasion

decision revision occasion persuasion collision division

provision erosion vision exclusion inclusion

3rd try

Time:

This timed reading exercise is for the pupil to improve his/her reading speed and fluency.   Ask the pupil to read the words as fast as they can. Record the time in the box. Repeat the exercise.

Dictation

Jack and Sam came to visit Viv. They watched 'Alien __ __ __ __ _____'. Grandpa said it was a special __ ____ __ _____ and switched off the __ __ __ __ __ __ _____. Viv made a __ __ __ __ _____ to dress up as an __ __ __ __ __ __ __ ____ __. Jack dressed up as an __ __ __ __ __. They had lots of epic battles with __ __ __ __ __ _____ __ and __ __ __ __ __ _____ s. Then little Sam got in the way and fell __ __ ____.

Jack and Sam came to visit Viv. They watched 'Alien <u>I</u> n <u>v</u> <u>a</u> <u>sion</u>'.
Grandpa said it was a special <u>o</u> <u>cc</u> <u>a</u> <u>sion</u> and switched off the
<u>t</u> <u>e</u> <u>l</u> <u>e</u> <u>v</u> <u>i</u> <u>sion</u>. Viv made a <u>d</u> <u>e</u> <u>c</u> <u>i</u> <u>sion</u> to dress up as an <u>a</u> <u>s</u> <u>t</u> <u>r</u> <u>o</u> <u>n</u> <u>au</u> <u>t</u>.
Jack dressed up as an <u>a</u> <u>l</u> <u>i</u> <u>e</u> <u>n</u>. They had lots of epic battles with
<u>c</u> <u>o</u> <u>ll</u> <u>i</u> <u>sion</u> s and <u>e</u> <u>x</u> <u>p</u> <u>l</u> <u>o</u> <u>sion</u> s. Then little Sam got in the way and fell
<u>o</u> <u>v</u> <u>er</u>.

Use the text at the bottom of the page for dictation. Fold the page on the dotted line. Dictate the passage to the pupil. Ask her/him to spell the missing words, writing a sound on each line. Explain that a longer line indicates a spelling with more than one letter e.g. <u>n</u> <u>igh</u> <u>t</u>. Ask the pupil to unfold the sheet and check his/her spellings. This sheet may be photocopied by the purchaser.

Level 4 Book 14: 'Alien Invasion' suffix <-sion>

Phonic patterns

Colour in the words with the suffix <-sion>

invasion	discussion	occasion	confusion
nature	vision	provision	division
reaction	mention	revision	enclosure
collision	treasure	pleasure	inclusion
explosion	decision	nature	pollution

Fold this sheet on the dotted line. Read the words in the column on the left. Listen to the sounds in the words. Colour in the lozenges with words that have the suffix <-sion>. Repeat this in the other columns. Unfold the sheet and check the correct words have been coloured in.

Level 4 Book 14: 'Alien Invasion'

Reading game

suffix ‹-sion›

Start

Finish

confusion

revision

vision

fusion

division

evasion

collision

explosion

occasion

erosion

invasion

decision

indecision

provision

conclusion

persuasion

inclusion

illusion

television

precision

excursion

exclusion

version

Play with counters and die. This sheet may be photocopied by the purchaser. © Phonic Books Ltd 2014

Spelling assessment

<-sion>
vision
division
confusion
occasion
explosion
collision
invasion

Reading game

Finish

Start